D1550725

VOGUE® KNITTING

KIDS KNITS

VOGUE KNITTING

KIDS KNITS

SIXTH&SPRING BOOKS
NEW YORK

SIXTH&SPRING BOOKS
233 Spring Street
New York, New York 10013

Library of Congress Cataloging-in-Publication Data

Vogue knitting kids knits / [editor, Trisha Malcolm].
        p. cm. -- (Vogue knitting on the go!)
        ISBN 1-931543-13-5
        1. Knitting--Patterns. 2. Children's clothing. I. Title: Kids knits. II. Malcolm, Trisha,
1960- III. Series.

    TT825 .V626 2002
    746.43'20432--dc21   2002021150

                    Manufactured in China

                    1 3 5 7 9 10 8 6 4 2

                        First Edition

TABLE OF CONTENTS

INTRODUCTION

Think there's no room in your busy schedule to knit? Think again. After all, knitting is the perfect portable project. You can take out your needles just about anywhere, anytime. Slip in a few stitches at your child's little league game, finish a row or two at the playground or stitch away on a morning commute.

Kids' knits are perfect for a life spent on the move. The pieces for the projects in this book are small, so you can tote your work-in-progress along wherever your travels take you. They also work up fast, so there's no need to worry that the recipient of your knitting talents will have outgrown your creation before it's off the needles.

Best of all, knitting for kids is fun. Creating for little ones gives you the freedom to go a little crazy with color, indulge in a bit of whimsy, or try out one of those fabulously textured new yarns. Small-scale projects like the ones on these pages also give you the opportunity to give new stitch patterns and techniques a whirl without a big investment in time or dollars. Let your imagination soar, your kids—and your soul—will love you for it.

So get in touch with your inner child, grab your needles and get set to **KNIT ON THE GO!**

THE BASICS

Knitting a garment or a personal object for a child is always a heartfelt production. By the time a child reaches the age of four, he or she has very specific ideas about what they prefer to wear. When you knit a precious gift for a growing child, you need to take into consideration the individuality of that child.

We have gathered together twenty designs that reflect the special personalities of the designers who created them as well as the recipients who will wear them. With the appropriate materials, concise, easy-to-follow instructions, and a clear idea of your child's tastes, you're ready to create beautiful designs, fashioned straight from the heart.

SIZING

Most of the garments in this book are written for sizes 4, 6, 8, and 10, allowing extra ease for your child to grow into the garment. Since children's measurements change so rapidly, it is best to measure your child or a sweater that fits well to determine which size to make.

YARN SELECTION

For an exact reproduction of the projects photographed, use the yarn listed in the "Materials" section of the pattern. We've chosen yarns that are readily available in the U.S. and Canada at the time of print-ing. The Resources list on pages 94 and 95 provides addresses of yarn distributors. Contact them for the name of a retailer in your area.

YARN SUBSTITUTION

You may wish to substitute yarns. Perhaps you view small-scale projects as a chance to incorporate leftovers from your yarn stash, or the yarn specified may not be available in your area. You'll need to knit to the given gauge to obtain the knitted measurements with a substitute yarn (see "Gauge" on page 11). Be sure to consider how the fiber content of the substitute yarn will affect the comfort and the ease of care of your projects.

To facilitate yarn substitution, *Vogue Knitting* grades yarn by the standard stitch gauge obtained in stockinette stitch. You'll find a grading number in the "Materials" section of the pattern, immediately following the fiber type of the yarn. Look for a substitute yarn that falls into the same category. The suggested needle size and gauge on the yarn label should be comparable to that on the "Yarn Symbols" chart (see page 14).

After you've successfully gauge-swatched a substitute yarn, you'll need to figure out how much of the substitute yarn the project requires. First, find the

GAUGE

It is always important to knit a gauge swatch, and it is even more so with garments to ensure proper fit.

Patterns usually state gauge over a 4"/10cm span; however, it's beneficial to make a larger test swatch. This gives a more precise stitch gauge, a better idea of the appearance and drape of the knitted fabric, and a chance for you to familiarize yourself with the stitch pattern.

The type of needles used—straight or double-pointed, wood or metal—will influence gauge, so knit your swatch with the needles you plan to use for the project. Measure gauge as illustrated. Try different needle sizes until your sample measures the required number of stitches and rows. *To get fewer stitches to the inch/cm, use larger needles; to get more stitches to the inch/cm, use smaller needles.*

Knitting in the round may tighten the gauge, so if you measured the gauge on a flat swatch, take another gauge reading after you begin knitting. When the piece measures at least 2"/5cm, lay it flat and measure over the stitches in the center of the piece, as the side stitches may be distorted.

It's a good idea to keep your gauge swatch in order to test blocking and cleaning methods.

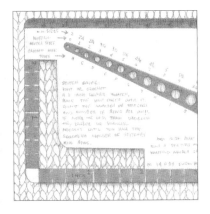

total length of the original yarn in the pattern (multiply number of balls by yards/meters per ball). Divide this figure by the new yards/meters per ball (listed on the yarn label). Round up to the next whole number. The answer is the number of balls required.

FOLLOWING CHARTS

Charts are a convenient way to follow colorwork, cable, and other stitch patterns at a glance. When knitting back and forth in rows, read charts from right to left on right side (RS) rows and from left to right on wrong side (WS) rows, repeating any stitch and row repeats as directed in the pattern. When knitting in the round, read charts from right to left on every round. Posting a self-adhesive note under your working row is an easy way to keep track of your place.

COLORWORK KNITTING

Two main types of colorwork are explored in this book: intarsia and stranding.

Intarsia

Intarsia is accomplished with separate bobbins of individual colors. Use this method for large blocks of color. When changing colors, always pick up the new color and wrap it around the old color to prevent holes.

Stranding

When motifs are closely placed, color-work is accomplished by stranding along two or more colors per row, creating floats on the wrong side of the fabric. This technique is sometimes called Fair Isle knitting after the traditional Fair Isle patterns that are composed of small motifs with frequent color changes.

To keep an even tension and prevent holes while knitting, pick up yarns alternately over and under one another across or around. While knitting, stretch the stitches on the needle slightly wider than the length of the float at the back to keep work from puckering.

When changing colors at the beginning of rows or rounds, carry yarn along for a few rows only, or cut yarn and rejoin when needed. It is important to keep the floats small and neat so they don't catch on small fingers when the garment is pulled on.

BLOCKING

Blocking is a crucial finishing step in the knitting process. It is the best way to shape pattern pieces and smooth knitted edges in preparation for sewing together. Most garments retain their shape if the blocking stages in the instructions are followed carefully. Choose a blocking method according to the instructions on the yarn care label, and when in doubt, test-block your gauge swatch.

Wet Block Method

Using rust-proof pins, pin pieces to measurements on a flat surface and lightly dampen using a spray bottle. Allow to dry before removing pins.

Steam Block Method

With wrong sides facing, pin pieces. Steam lightly, holding the iron 2"/5cm above the knitting. Do not press or it will flatten stitches.

FRINGE

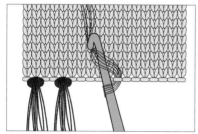

Simple fringe: Cut yarn twice desired length plus extra for knotting. On wrong side, insert hook from front to back through piece and over folded yarn. Pull yarn through. Draw ends through and tighten. Trim yarn.

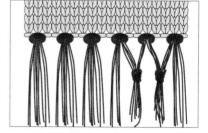

Knotted fringe: After working a simple fringe (it should be longer to allow for extra knotting), take one half of the strands from each fringe and knot them with half the strands from the neighboring fringe.

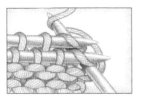
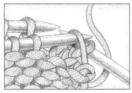
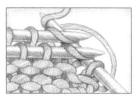

1 With RS placed together, hold pieces on two parallel needles. Insert a third needle knitwise into the first stitch of each needle, and wrap the yarn around the needle as if to knit.

2 Knit these two stitches together, and slip them off the needles. *Knit the next two stitches together in the same manner.

3 Slip the first stitch on the third needle over the second stitch and off the needle. Repeat from the * in Step 2 across the row until all stitches have been bound off.

THE KITCHENER STITCH

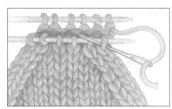

1 Insert tapestry needle purlwise (as shown) through first stitch on front needle. Pull yarn through, leaving that stitch on knitting needle.

2 Insert tapestry needle knitwise (as shown) through first stitch on back needle. Pull yarn through, leaving stitch on knitting needle.

3 Insert tapestry needle knitwise through first stitch on front needle, slip stitch off needle and insert tapestry needle purlwise (as shown) through next stitch on front needle. Pull yarn through, leaving this stitch on needle.

4 Insert tapestry needle purlwise through first stitch on back needle. Slip stitch off needle and insert tapestry needle knitwise (as shown) through next stitch on back needle. Pull yarn through, leaving this stitch on needle.
Repeat steps 3 and 4 until all stitches on both front and back needles have been grafted. Fasten off and weave in end.

Refer to the yarn label for the recommended cleaning method. Many of the projects in the book can be either washed by hand, or in the machine on a gentle or wool cycle, using lukewarm water with a mild detergent. Do not agitate or soak for more than 10 minutes. Rinse gently with tepid water, then fold in a towel and gently press the water out. Lay flat to dry, away from excess heat and light. Check the yarn label for any specific care instructions such as dry cleaning or tumble drying.

YARN SYMBOLS

① **Fine Weight**
(29-32 stitches per 4"/10cm)
Includes baby and fingering yarns, and some of the heavier crochet cottons. The range of needle sizes is 0-4 (2-3.5mm).

② **Lightweight**
(25-28 stitches per 4"/10cm)
Includes sport yarn, sock yarn, UK 4-ply, and lightweight DK yarns. The range of needle sizes is 3-6 (3.25-4mm).

③ **Medium Weight**
(21-24 stitches per 4"/10cm)
Includes DK and worsted, the most commonly used knitting yarns. The range of needle sizes is 6-9 (4-5.5mm).

④ **Medium-heavy Weight**
(17-20 stitches per 4"/10cm)
Also called heavy worsted or Aran. The range of needle sizes is 8-10 (5-6mm).

⑤ **Bulky Weight**
(13-16 stitches per 4"/10cm)
Also called chunky. Includes heavier Icelandic yarns. The range of needle sizes is 10-11 (6-8mm).

⑥ **Extra-bulky Weight**
(9-12 stitches per 4"/10cm)
The heaviest yarns available. The range of needle sizes is 11 and up (8mm and up).

KNITTING TERMS AND ABBREVIATIONS

approx approximately

beg begin(ning)

bind off Used to finish an edge and keep stitches from unraveling. Lift the first stitch over the second, the second over the third, etc. (UK: cast off)

cast on A foundation row of stitches placed on the needle in order to begin knitting.

CC contrast color

ch chain(s)

cm centimeter(s)

cont continu(e)(ing)

dc double crochet (UK: tr–treble)

dec decrease(ing)–Reduce the stitches in a row (knit 2 together).

dpn double-pointed needle(s)

foll follow(s)(ing)

g gram(s)

garter stitch Knit every row. Circular knitting: knit one round, then purl one round.

hdc half double crochet (UK: htr–half treble)

inc increase(ing)–Add stitches in a row (knit into the front and back of a stitch).

k knit

k2tog knit 2 stitches together

LH left-hand

lp(s) loop(s)

m meter(s)

M1 make one stitch–With the needle tip, lift the strand between last stitch worked and next stitch on the left-hand needle and knit into the back of it. One stitch has been added.

MC main color

mm millimeter(s)

no stitch On some charts, "no stitch" is indicated with shaded spaces where stitches have been decreased or not yet made. In such cases, work the stitches of the chart, skipping over the "no stitch" spaces.

oz ounce(s)

p purl

p2tog purl 2 stitches together

pat(s) pattern

pick up and knit (purl) Knit (or purl) into the loops along an edge.

pm place markers–Place or attach a loop of contrast yarn or purchased stitch marker as indicated.

psso pass slip stitch(es) over

rem remain(s)(ing)

rep repeat

rev St st reverse stockinette stitch–Purl right-side rows, knit wrong-side rows. Circular knitting: purl all rounds. (UK: reverse stocking stitch)

rnd(s) round(s)

RH right-hand

RS right side(s)

sc single crochet (UK: dc–double crochet)

sk skip

SKP Slip 1, knit 1, pass slip stitch over knit 1.

SK2P Slip 1, knit 2 together, pass slip stitch over the knit 2 together.

sl slip–An unworked stitch made by passing a stitch from the left-hand to the right-hand needle as if to purl.

sl st slip stitch (UK: sc–single crochet)

ssk slip, slip, knit–Slip next 2 stitches knitwise, one at a time, to right-hand needle. Insert tip of left-hand needle into fronts of these stitches from left to right. Knit them together. One stitch has been decreased.

sssk Slip next 3 sts knitwise, one at a time, to right-hand needle. Insert tip of left-hand needle into fronts of these stitches from left to right. Knit them together. Two stitches have been decreased.

st(s) stitch(es)

St st Stockinette stitch–Knit right-side rows, purl wrong-side rows. Circular knitting: knit all rounds. (UK: stocking stitch)

tbl through back of loop

tog together

WS wrong side(s)

wyib with yarn in back

wyif with yarn in front

work even Continue in pattern without increasing or decreasing. (UK: work straight)

yd yard(s)

yo yarn over–Make a new stitch by wrapping the yarn over the right-hand needle. (UK: yfwd, yon, yrn)

* = Repeat directions following * as many times as indicated.

[ ] = Repeat directions inside brackets as many times as indicated.

This oversized coat with hood, extra long sleeves and set-in pockets will keep your child warm and toasty even in the coldest weather. Wide horseshoe cables accent the front of this otherwise garter stitch garment. Designed by Kristin Nicholas.

SIZES

Instructions are written for size 4. Changes for 6, 8 and 10 are in parentheses.

KNITTED MEASUREMENTS

▦ Chest (buttoned) 28 (32, 36, 38)"/71 (81, 91.5, 96.5)cm

▦ Length 16½ (17½, 18½, 19½)"/42 (44.5, 47, 49.5)cm

▦ Upper arm 12½ (13½, 14½, 15½)"/31.5 (34, 37, 39)cm

MATERIALS

▦ 8 (9, 10, 11) 2oz/57g skeins (each approx 140yd/128m) of Green Mountain Spinnery *Mountain Mohair* (wool④) in #5-D1 day lily

▦ One pair each sizes 5 and 7 (3.75 and 4.5mm) needles *or size to obtain gauge*

▦ Cable needle

▦ Stitch holders

▦ Stitch markers

▦ 5 (5, 6, 6) ¾"/19mm buttons.i

GAUGE

17 sts and 34 rows to 4"/10cm over garter st using size 7 (4.5mm) needles.
Take time to check gauge.

CABLE PANEL

(over 12 sts)

Row 1 (RS) K12.

Row 2 P12.

Row 3 Sl 3 sts to cn and hold to *back*, k3, k3 from cn, sl 3 sts to cn and hold to *front*, k3, k3 from cn.

Rows 4 and 6 P3, k6, p3.

Rows 5 and 7 K3, p6, k3

Row 8 Rep row 4.

Rep rows 1-8 for cable panel.

BACK

With smaller needles, cast on 60 (68, 77, 81) sts. Work in garter st for 2"/5cm. Change to larger needles. Cont in garter st until piece measures 16½ (17½, 18½, 19½)"/42 (44.5, 47, 49.5)cm from beg.

Neck and shoulder shaping

Bind off 18 (22, 25, 27) sts at beg of next 2 rows. Place rem 24 (24, 27, 27) sts on a holder for back neck.

POCKETS

With larger needles, cast on 13 (13, 15, 15) sts. Work in garter st for 3½ (3½, 4½, 4½)"/9 (9, 11.5, 11.5)cm, end with a WS row. Place sts on a holder.

LEFT FRONT

With smaller needles, cast on 33 (37, 42, 44) sts.

Beg cable panel

Row 1 (RS) K 19 (23, 28, 30) sts, pm, work 12 sts in cable panel, pm, k2. Cont in pats as established, working sts each side of cable panel in garter st, until piece measures 2"/5cm. Change to larger needles. Cont as established until piece measures 5½ (5½, 6½, 6½)"/14 (14, 16.5, 16.5)cm from beg, end with a RS row.

Pocket placement

Next row (WS) Work 15 (17, 18, 19) sts, bind off next 13 (13, 15, 15) sts for pocket opening, work to end. **Next row (RS)** Work 5 (7, 9, 10) sts, with same strand of yarn work 13 (13, 15, 15) pocket sts, work to end. Cont as established until piece measures 14½ (15½, 16½, 17½)"/37 (39, 42, 44.5)cm from beg, end with a RS row.

Neck shaping

Next row (WS) Bind off 11 (11, 13, 13) sts, work to end. Dec 1 st from neck edge every other row 4 times—18 (22, 25, 27) sts. Work even until piece measures same as back. Bind off.

RIGHT FRONT

With smaller needles, cast on 33 (37, 42, 44) sts.

Beg cable panel

Row 1 (RS) K2, pm, work 12 sts in cable panel, pm, k 19 (23, 28, 30) sts. Cont to work as for left front to pocket placement.

Pocket placement

Next row (WS) Work 5 (7, 9, 10) sts, bind off next 13 (13, 15, 15) sts for pocket opening, work to end. **Next row (RS)** Work 15 (17, 18, 19) sts, with same strand of yarn, work 13 (13, 15, 15) pocket sts, work to end. Cont to work as for left front, reversing neck shaping.

SLEEVES

With smaller needles, cast on 32 (34, 36, 36) sts. Work in garter st for 2"/5cm. Change to larger needles. Cont in garter st and inc 1 st each side every 6th row 0 (0, 2, 8) times, then every 8th row 11 (12, 11, 7) times—54 (58, 62, 66) sts. Work even until piece measures 13 (14, 15, 16)"/33 (35.5, 38, 40.5)cm from beg. Bind off.

FINISHING

Block pieces to measurements. Sew

shoulder seams. Sew pockets in place.

Buttonband

With smaller needles, cast on 5 sts. Work in garter st until piece measures 14½ (15½, 16½, 17½)"/37 (39, 42, 44.5)cm from beg. Bind off. Mark placement of 5 (5, 6, 6) buttons on band, with first and last ¾"/2cm from top and bottom edges and 3 (3, 4, 4) spaced evenly between. Sew to left front edge.

Buttonhole band

Work as for buttonband, working buttonholes opposite markers. **Buttonhole row** K2, yo, k2tog, k1. **Next row** K5. Cont to work as for buttonband. Sew to right front edge.

Hood

With RS facing and larger needles, pick up and k 64 (66, 71, 73) sts along entire neck edge. Work in garter st for 10 (10½, 11, 11½)"/25.5 (26.5, 28, 29)cm. Bind off. Sew hood seam. Place markers at 6¼ (6¾, 7¼, 7¾)"/16 (17, 18.5, 19.5)cm down from shoulders. Sew sleeves to armholes between markers. Sew side and sleeve seams. Fold back cuffs. Sew on buttons.

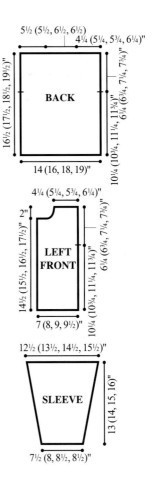

Debbie Bliss, renowned children's knitwear designer, created this sweatshirt featuring a cool stockinette hood, slanted pockets and side slits. Designed with comfort and style in mind, this essential pullover is a must-have addition to your child's wardrobe.

SIZES

Instructions are written for size 4. Changes for 6, 8 and 10 are in parentheses.

KNITTED MEASUREMENTS

Chest 30 (33, 36, 39)"/76 (84, 91.5, 99)cm

Length 16 (17, 18, 19)"/40.5 (43, 45.5, 48)cm

Upper arm 13 (14, 15, 16)"/33 (35.5, 38, 40.5)cm

MATERIALS

12 (13, 14, 16) 1¾oz/50g balls (each approx 86yd/79m) of Debbie Bliss Yarns/KFI *Merino Aran* (wool④) in #205 blue

One pair each sizes 7 and 8 (4.5 and 5mm) needles *or size to obtain gauge*

Stitch holders

GAUGE

20 sts and 26 rows to 4"/10cm over St st using size 8 (5mm) needles.
Take time to check gauge.

STITCH GLOSSARY

CR2R

Sk first st on LH needle and k into 2nd st, then k first st; sl both sts from needle.

CROSS-STITCH RIB

Row 1 (RS) K3, *p2, CR2R, p2, k2; rep from *, end p2, CR2R, p2, k3.
Row 2 P3, *k2, p2; rep from *, end k2, p3.
Rep rows 1 and 2 for cross-stitch rib.

BACK

With smaller needles, cast on 74 (82, 90, 98) sts.

Beg rib pat

Rows 1-4 Knit. **Row 5 (RS)** K4, *p2, k2; rep from * across, end p2, k4. **Row 6** K2, *p2, k2; rep from * to end. Rep last 2 rows 2 (2, 3, 3) times more, then rep rows 1-4 once. Change to larger needles and cont in St st until piece measures 9½ (10, 10½, 11)"/24 (25.5, 26.5, 28)cm from beg, end with a WS row.

Yoke

Next (inc) row K 6 (5, 5, 4), [M1, k 7 (8, 9, 10) sts] 9 times, end M1, k 5 (5, 4, 4)—84 (92, 100, 108) sts. **Next 3 rows** Knit. Work in cross-stitch rib until piece measures 16 (17, 18, 19)"/40.5 (43, 45.5, 48)cm from beg, end with a WS row.

Neck and shoulder shaping

Bind off 12 (14, 16, 17) sts at beg of next 2 rows, then 13 (14, 16, 18) sts at beg of next 2 rows. Bind off rem 34 (36, 36, 38) sts for back neck.

POCKET LINING

With larger needles, cast on 60 (64, 68, 72) sts. Work in St st for 12 (12, 14, 16) rows, end with a WS row. Place sts on a holder.

FRONT

Work as for back until 12 (12, 14, 16) rows of St st have been completed, end with a WS row.

Pocket shaping

Next row (RS) Work first 7 (9, 11, 13) sts and place on a holder, bind off next 4 sts, work 56 (60, 64, 68) sts, place last 7 (9, 11, 13) sts on a holder. **Next row (WS)** Bind off 4 sts, work to end—52 (56, 60, 64) sts. Dec 1 st each side every row 17 (18, 19, 20) times—18 (20, 22, 24) sts. Work 1 (0, 1, 0) more row. Place sts on a holder for pocket.

Pocket joining

Next row (RS) K first 7 (9, 11, 13) sts from holder, k 60 (64, 68, 72) sts of pocket lining, k last 7 (9, 11, 13) sts from holder—74 (82, 90, 98) sts. Beg with a p row, work even for 17 (17, 19, 19) rows, end with a WS row. Place 18 (20, 22, 24) pocket sts on a spare needle. **Next row (RS)** K 28 (31, 34, 37) sts, with pocket sts in front of lining sts and needles parallel, k 1 st from front needle tog with 1 st from back needle across next 18 (20, 22, 24) sts, work to end—74 (82, 90, 98) sts. Cont to work as for back until piece measures 13 (14, 15, 16)"/33 (35.5, 38, 40.5)cm from beg, end with a WS row.

Neck and shoulder shaping

Next row (RS) Work 34 (37, 41, 44) sts, join another ball of yarn and bind off 16 (18, 18, 20) sts, work to end. Working both sides at once, dec 1 st at each neck edge *every* row 9 times—25 (28, 32, 35) sts each side. Work until piece measures same length as back to shoulder. Shape shoulder as for back.

SLEEVES

With smaller needles, cast on 42 (46, 46, 50) sts. Work in k2, p2 rib for 2"/5cm, end with a WS row. Change to larger needles. Cont in St st. Inc 1 st each side every 4th row 4 (8, 8, 8) times, then every 6th row 4 (2, 2, 4) times—58 (66, 66, 74) sts. Work even until piece measures 8½ (9½, 10, 11)"/21.5 (24, 25.5, 28)cm from beg, end with a RS row. **Next (inc) row** K 4 (5, 5, 6), [M1, k 7 (8, 8, 9)] 7 times, end M1, k 5—66 (74, 74, 82) sts. **Next 3 rows** Knit, inc 1 st each side of last row—68 (76, 76, 84) sts. Work in cross-stitch rib and inc 1 st each side (working incs into pat st) on next row, then every 3rd row 2 (1, 4, 3) times more—74 (80, 86, 92) sts. Work even until piece measures 11(12, 13, 14)"/28 (30.5, 33, 35.5)cm from beg, end with a WS row. Bind off.

HOOD

With larger needles, cast on 92 (98, 104, 110) sts. Work in St st until piece measures 10½ (11½, 12, 12½)"/26.5 (29, 30.5, 31.5)cm from beg. Bind off. Fold in half, RS tog and sew bound-off edge.

Edging

With RS facing and smaller needles, pick

up and k 106 (110, 118, 126) sts evenly spaced along front edge. Work in k2, p2 rib for 4 rows. Bind off loosely in rib.

Block pieces to measurements. Sew bottom edge of lining in place.

Pocket edging

With RS facing and smaller needles, pick up and k 26 (26, 30, 30) sts along pocket edge. Work in k2, p2 rib for 3 rows. Bind off loosely in rib. Sew side edges of edging in place. Sew shoulder seams. Sew on hood, easing in fullness around neck. Place markers at 6½ (7, 7½, 8)"/16.5 (17.5, 19, 20)cm down from shoulders. Sew sleeves to armholes between markers. Sew side seams, leaving lower edge rib unsewn for slits. Sew sleeve seams.

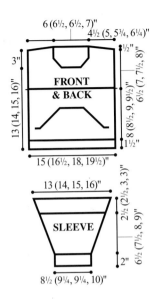

6 (6½, 6½, 7)"
4½ (5, 5¾, 6¼)"
½"
3"
13 (14, 15, 16)"
FRONT & BACK
8 (8½, 9, 9½)"
6½ (7, 7½, 8)"
1½"
15 (16½, 18, 19½)"

13 (14, 15, 16)"
2½ (2½, 3, 3)"
SLEEVE
6½ (7½, 8, 9)"
2"
8½ (9¼, 9¼, 10)"

Simplicity and vibrant colors make this basic pullover by Jil Eaton quick and fun to knit. Shoulder seams are knit together so that the ridge is exposed on the right side—Jil's signature.

SIZES

Instructions are written for size 4. Changes for 6, 8 and 10 are in parentheses.

KNITTED MEASUREMENTS

■ Chest 31 (33, 34, 36½)"/78.5 (83.5, 86.5, 92.5)cm
■ Length 13 (14¾, 14¾, 16¾)"/33 (37.5, 37.5, 42.5)cm
■ Upper arm 13 (13½, 14, 15)"/33 (34, 35.5, 38)cm

MATERIALS

■ 3 (3, 4, 4) 1¾oz/50g hanks (each approx 85yd/78m) of Berroco, Inc. *Cotton Twist* (cotton/rayon③) in #839 0 black (MC)
■ 1 hank each in #8348 orange (A), #8311 red (B), #8335 blue (C) and #8306 turquoise (D)
■ One pair size 5 (3.75mm) needles or *size to obtain gauge*
■ One set (4) size 5 (3.75mm) dpn
■ Size 5 (3.75mm) circular needle, 16"/40cm long
■ Stitch holders

GAUGE

21 sts and 28 rows to 4"/10cm over St st using size 5 (3.75mm) needles.
Take time to check gauge.

BACK

With straight needles and MC, cast on 70 (74, 78, 84) sts. Work in St st for 5 (7, 7, 7) rows, inc 12 sts evenly spaced across last row, end with a RS row—82 (86, 90, 96) sts. **Next row (WS)** Knit for turning ridge.

Stripe Pat

Cont in St st as foll: 7 (8, 8, 9) rows each in MC, A, MC, B, MC, C, MC, D, MC, A, MC, B and MC—91 (104, 104, 117) rows; piece should measure 13 (14¾, 14¾, 16¾)"/33 (37.5, 37.5, 42.5)cm above turning ridge, end with a WS row.

Neck and shoulder shaping

Next row (RS) K 30 (32, 33, 35) sts and place on a holder, k 22 (22, 24, 26) sts for back neck and place on a holder, k rem 30 (32, 33, 35) sts and place on a holder.

FRONT

Work as for back until 6 (6, 6, 8) rows of 6th MC stripe have been completed, end with a WS row. Piece should measure 10¾ (12¼, 12¼, 14)"/27 (31, 31, 35.5)cm above turning ridge.

Neck shaping

Next row (RS) Work 34 (36, 37, 39) sts, join 2nd ball of MC and bind off center 14 (14, 16, 18) sts, work to end. Working both sides at once, dec 1 st from each neck edge every other row 4 times. Work even until same length as back. Place 30 (32, 33, 35) sts each side on holders for shoulders.

SLEEVES

With straight needles and MC, cast on 40

(42, 44, 46) sts. Work in St st for 5 (7, 7, 7) rows, inc 4 sts evenly spaced across last row, end with a RS row—44 (46, 48, 50) sts. **Next row (WS)** Knit for turning ridge.

Stripe Pat

Cont in St st as foll: work 7 (8, 8, 9) rows each in MC, A, MC, B, MC, C and MC, AT THE SAME TIME, when 6 rows of first MC stripe are completed, beg sleeve shaping. Inc 1 st each side every other row 9 (8, 8, 7) times, then every 4th row 5 (6, 7, 9) times—72 (74, 78, 82) sts. Work even until stripe pat is completed—49 (56, 56, 63) rows and piece should measure 7 (8, 8, 9)"/17.5 (20, 20, 23)cm above turning ridge. Bind off.

FINISHING

Block pieces to measurements. Join first shoulder tog as foll: With WS of pieces tog, sl shoulder sts to 2 dpn. With 3rd dpn, and shoulder sts parallel, k 1 st from back dpn with 1 st from front dpn and bind off while working tog for three-needle bind off. Rep for rem shoulder.

NECKBAND

With RS facing, circular needle and MC, pick up and k 84 (86, 90, 94) sts evenly around neck. Join and work in k1, p1 rib for 4 (4, 6, 6) rows. Bind off loosely in rib. Place markers at 6½ (6¾, 7, 7½)"/16.5 (17, 17.5, 19)cm down from shoulders. Sew sleeves to armholes between markers. Sew side and sleeve seams. Fold lower edge and sleeve hems to WS at turning ridges and sew in place.

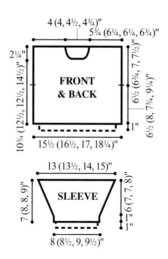

4 (4, 4½, 4¾)"
5¾ (6¼, 6¼, 6¾)"
2¼"
10¾ (12½, 12½, 14½)"
FRONT & BACK
6½ (6¾, 7, 7½)"
6½ (8, 7¾, 9¼)"
1"
15½ (16½, 17, 18¼)"

13 (13½, 14, 15)"
7 (8, 8, 9)"
SLEEVE
6 (6, 7, 8)"
1"
1"
8 (8½, 9, 9½)"

FLEECE HOODED JACKET

Just fur you

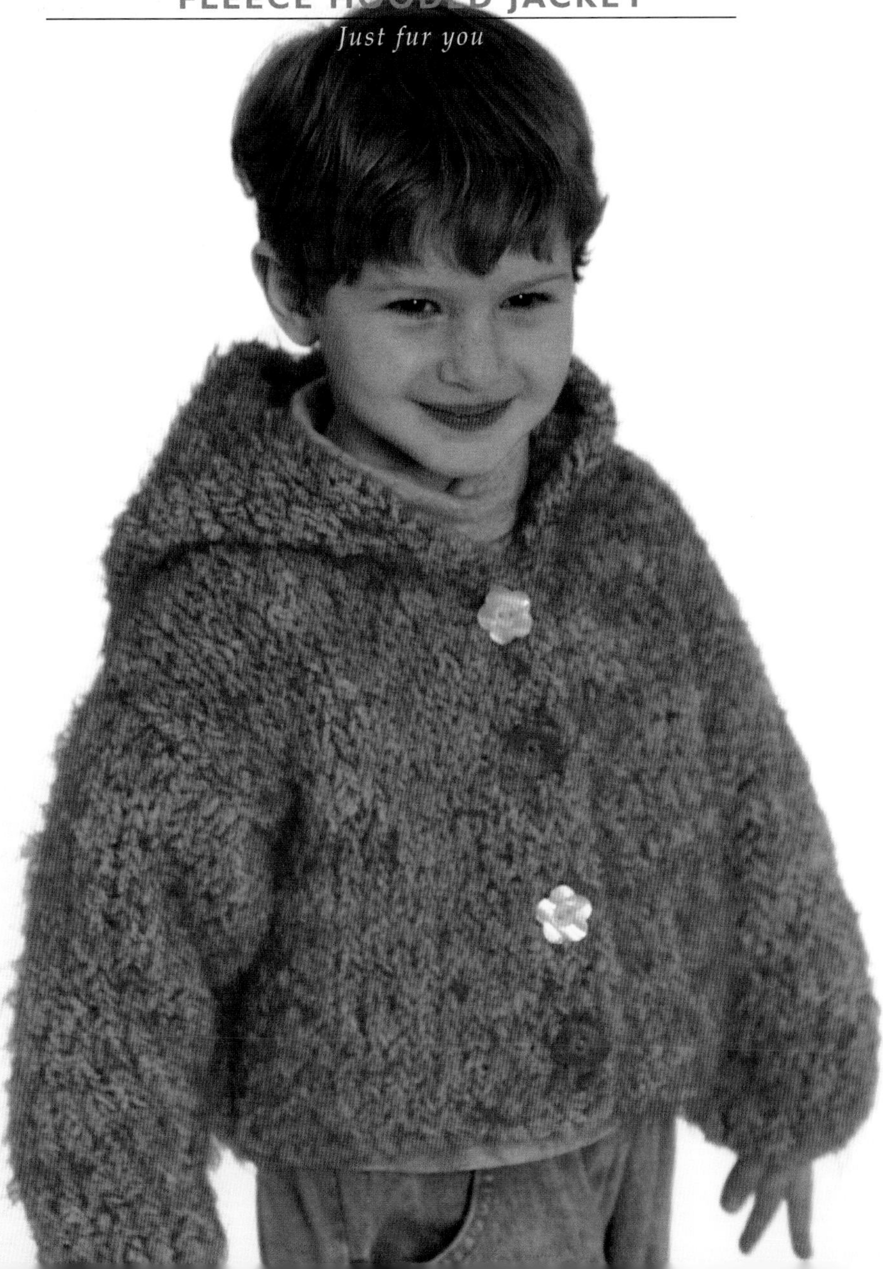

A combination of shag-cut and a bright furry yarn create a marled look on this plush jacket designed by Veronica Manno. Add decorative buttons to spice up the simple silhouette.

SIZES

Instructions are written for size 4. Changes for 6, 8 and 10 are in parentheses.

KNITTED MEASUREMENTS

▨ Chest (buttoned) 31 (33, 35, 37)"/78.5 (83.5, 89, 94)cm
▨ Length 13 (14, 15, 16)"/33 (35.5, 38, 40.5)cm
▨ Upper arm 14 (15, 16, 17)"/35.5 (38, 40.5, 43)cm

MATERIALS

▨ 6 (8, 9, 10) 1¾oz/50g hanks (each approx 47yd/43m) of K1C2, LLC *Flureece* (wool/nylon④) in #460 bright yellow (A)
▨ 3 (4, 4, 5) 1¾oz/50g hanks (each approx 180yd/165m) of Trendsetter Yarns *Voila* (polyamide④) in #10 pink (B)
▨ One pair size 13 (9mm) needles *or size to obtain gauge*
▨ 4 (4, 5, 5) 1"/25mm buttons

GAUGE

8 sts and 14 rows to 4"/10cm over St st using 1 strand each A and B held tog and size 13 (9mm) needles.
Take time to check gauge.

Note One strand of A and B are held tog throughout.

BACK

Cast on 31 (33, 35, 37) sts. Work in St st for 13 (14, 15, 16)"/33 (35.5, 38, 40.5)cm. Bind off all sts.

LEFT FRONT

Cast on 17 (18, 19, 20) sts. Work in St st for 11 (12, 13, 14)"/28 (30.5, 33, 35.5)cm, end with a RS row.

Neck shaping

Next row (WS) Bind off 5 (5, 6, 6) sts (neck edge), work to end. Dec 1 st from neck edge *every* row twice—10 (11, 11, 12) sts. Work even until same length as back. Bind off. Mark placement of 4 (4, 5, 5) buttons, with first and last 1¼"/3cm from top and bottom edges and 2 (2, 3, 3) spaced evenly between.

RIGHT FRONT

Work as for left front, reversing shaping and making buttonholes opposite markers on left front as foll: **Next row (RS)** K2, bind off next st, work to end. On next row p to bound-off st, yo, p 2.

SLEEVES

Cast on 16 sts. Work in St st, inc 1 st each side every 4th row 2 (3, 4, 5) times, then every 6th row 4 times—28 (30, 32, 34) sts. Work even until piece measures 11 (12, 13, 14)"/28 (30.5, 33, 35.5)cm from beg. Bind off.

Block pieces to measurements. Sew shoulder seams.

HOOD

With RS facing, pick up and k 31 (31, 33, 35) sts evenly along neck edge. Beg with a p row, work in St st for 3 rows, end with a WS row.

Hood shaping

Inc row 1 (RS) K 15 (15, 16, 17), M1, k1, M1, k 15 (15, 16, 17)—33 (33, 35, 37) sts. Work even for 3 rows. **Inc row 2 (RS)** K 16 (16, 17, 18), M1, k1, M1, k 16 (16, 17, 18)—35 (35, 37, 39) sts. Work even for 5 rows. **Inc row 3 (RS)** K 17 (17, 18, 19), M1, k1, M1, k 17 (17, 18, 19)—37 (37, 39, 41) sts. Work even for 5 rows. *For sizes 4 and 6 only* **Inc row 4 (RS)** K 18 (18), M1, k1, M1, k 18 (18)—39 (39) sts. *For all sizes* Work even until hood measures 10 (10½, 11, 12)"/25.5 (26.5, 28, 30.5)cm from beg. Bind off. Sew top of hood seam.

Place markers at 7 (7½, 8, 8½)"/17.5 (19, 20.5, 21.5)cm down from shoulders. Sew sleeves to armholes between markers. Sew side and sleeve seams. Sew on buttons.

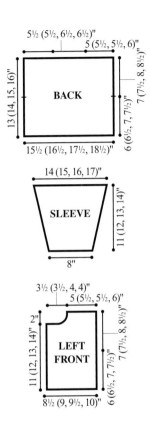

BACK
5½ (5½, 6½, 6½)"
5 (5½, 5½, 6)"
13 (14, 15, 16)"
7 (7½, 8, 8½)"
6 (6½, 7, 7½)"
15½ (16½, 17½, 18½)"

SLEEVE
14 (15, 16, 17)"
11 (12, 13, 14)"
8"

LEFT FRONT
3½ (3½, 4, 4)"
5 (5½, 5½, 6)"
2"
11 (12, 13, 14)"
7 (7½, 8, 8½)"
6 (6½, 7, 7½)"
8½ (9, 9½, 10)"

Delicate floral motifs and allover purl-stitch diamonds lend sophistication to this delicate cardigan. Pretty picot edging adorn the neckline, cuffs and hem. Designed by Kirstin Spurkland.

SIZES

Instructions are written for size 4. Changes for 6, 8 and 10 are in parentheses.

KNITTED MEASUREMENTS

Chest (buttoned) 27 (29, 31, 33)"/73.5 (73, 78.5, 83.5)cm

Length 11 (12, 13, 14)"/28 (30.5, 33, 35.5)cm

Upper arm 11 (12, 13, 14)"/ 28 (30.5, 33, 35.5)cm

MATERIALS

5 (6, 7, 8) 1¾oz/50g skeins (each approx 109yd/99m) of Dale of Norway *Heilo* (wool③) in #5532 lavender (MC)

1 (1, 2, 2) skeins in #5762 dk gray (A)

1 skein in #7032 green (B)

One pair each sizes 2, 3 and 4 (2.5, 3 and 3.5mm) needles *or size to obtain gauge*

Sizes 2, 3 and 4 (2.5, 3 and 3.5mm) circular needles, 24"/60cm long

Stitch holders

Four (4, 5, 5) 3/8"/10mm buttons

GAUGES

24 sts and 36 rows to 4"/10cm over diamond chart using size 3 (3mm) needles.

24 sts and 30 rows to 4"/10cm over St st and floral chart using size 4 (3.5mm) needles. *Take time to check gauges.*

Notes I Body is worked in one piece to armhole, then both fronts and back are worked separately to shoulder. **2** When changing colors, twist yarns on WS to prevent holes in work.

BODY

With size 2 (2.5mm) circular needle and MC, cast on 161 (173, 185, 197) sts. Work in St st for 6 rows, end with a WS row. Work picot row as foll: **Next row (RS)** K2, *yo, k2tog; rep from *, end k1. Beg with a p row, cont in St st for 6 rows more, end with a RS row. Change to size 4 (3.5mm) circular needle and B. **Next row (WS)** Purl.

Beg floral chart

Next row (RS) Beg with st 1 and work to st 14, then work 12-st rep (sts 15-26) 11 (12, 13, 14) times, then work sts 27-41 once. Cont as established through row 17. Change to size 3 (3mm) circular needle and MC. **Next row (WS)** Purl.

Beg diamond chart

Next row (RS) Beg with st 3 (1, 3, 1) and work to st 10, then work 8-st rep (sts 11-18) 18 (19, 21, 22) times, then sts 19-27 (19-29, 19-27, 19-29) once. Cont as established (rep rows 1-16) and work even until piece measures 6 (6½, 7, 7½)"/15 (16.5, 17.5, 19)cm from beg, end with a WS row.

Separate for fronts and back

Next row (RS) Work 40 (43, 46, 49) sts and place on holder for right front, work until there are 81 (87, 93, 99) sts for back, leave rem sts unworked for left front. Change to size 3 (3mm) straight needles and work back sts only for 1 row.

Armhole shaping

Cont on back sts in pat established, dec 1 st each side every other row 3 times—75 (81, 87, 93) sts. Work even until armhole measures 5 (5½, 6, 6½)"/12.5 (14, 15, 16.5)cm, end with a WS row.

Neck and shoulder shaping

Next row (RS) Work 23 (25, 27, 29) sts, place center 29 (31, 33, 35) sts on a holder for back neck, join 2nd skein of MC, work to end. Working both sides at once, dec 1 st at each neck edge every other row once—22 (24, 26, 28) sts each side. Work even until armhole measures 5½ (6, 6½, 7)"/14 (15, 16.5, 17.5)cm. Bind off each side.

RIGHT FRONT

Slip 40 (43, 46, 49) sts on right front holder to size 3 (3mm) straight needles and work for 1 row.

V-neck and armhole shaping

Next (dec) row (RS) K3, ssk (neck dec), work to end. Rep dec row every other row 14 (15, 16, 17) times more and AT SAME TIME, dec 1 st from armhole edge every other row 3 times. Work even on 22 (24, 26, 28) sts until same length as back. Bind off.

LEFT FRONT

Join MC to rem sts. Change to size 3 (3mm) straight needles and work even for 2 rows.

V-neck and armhole shaping

Next (dec) row (RS) Work to last 5 sts, k2tog (neck dec), k3. Rep dec row every other row 14 (15, 16, 17) times more and AT SAME TIME, dec 1 st at armhole edge every other row 3 times. Work even on 22 (24, 26, 28) sts until same length as back. Bind off.

SLEEVES

With size 2 (2.5mm) straight needles and MC, cast on 41 (41, 53, 53) sts. Work in St st for 6 rows, end with a WS row. **Next row (RS)** K2, *yo, k2tog; rep from *, end k1. Beg with a p row, cont in St st for 6 more rows, end with a RS row. Change to size 4 (3.5mm) straight needles and B. **Next row (WS)** Purl.

Beg floral chart

Next row (RS) Beg with st 1 and work to st 14, then work 12-st rep 1 (1, 2, 2) times, then work sts 27-41 once. Cont as established through row 17. Change to size 3 (3mm) straight needles and MC. **Next row (WS)** Purl.

Beg diamond chart

Row 1 (RS) Beg with st 3 (3, 1, 1) and work to st 10, then work 8-st rep 3 (3, 4, 4) times, then row sts 19-27 (19-27, 19-29, 19-29) once. Cont as established and inc 1 st each side (working incs into pat) every 4th row 0 (5, 0, 0) times, every 6th row 10

(11, 5, 10) times, then every 8th row 3 (0, 8, 6) times—67 (73, 79, 85) sts. Work even until piece measures 11½ (12½, 13½, 14½)"/29 (31.5, 34, 37)cm from beg.

Cap shaping

Dec 1 st each side every other row 3 times—-61 (67, 73, 79) sts. Bind off.

FINISHING

Block pieces to measurements. Sew shoulder seams. Fold bottom band to WS along picot row and sew in place. On right front, mark placement of 4 (4, 5, 5) buttonholes, with first ¾"/2cm from lower edge, the last at beg of neck shaping and 2 (2, 3, 3) spaced evenly between.

Neckband

With RS facing, size 2 (2.5mm) circular needle and MC, pick up and k 183 (205, 221, 235) sts evenly spaced along front and back neck edges. Beg with a p row, work in St st for 2 rows, end with a RS row. **Buttonhole row (WS)** *P to marker, yo, p2tog; rep from * to end. Work for 2 more rows. **Next row (RS)** K2, *yo, k2tog; rep from *, end k1. Beg with a p row, work in St st for 2 rows, end with a RS row. Rep buttonhole row, then work for 2 more rows. Bind off loosely. Set in sleeves. Sew sleeve seams. Fold rem bands to WS along picot row and sew in place. Sew on buttons.

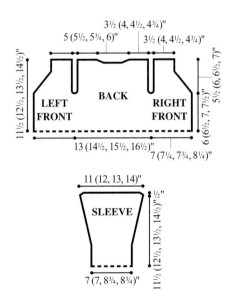

FLORAL CHART

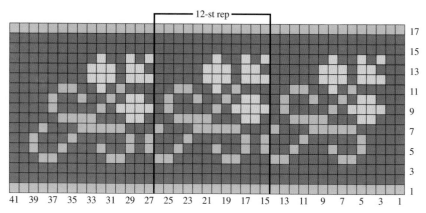

12-st rep

41 39 37 35 33 31 29 27 25 23 21 19 17 15 13 11 9 7 5 3 1

17 15 13 11 9 7 5 3 1

Color Key

Lavender (MC)

Dk grey (A)

Green (B)

Stitch Key

☐ K on RS, p on WS

Ⅰ P on RS, k on WS

DIAMOND CHART

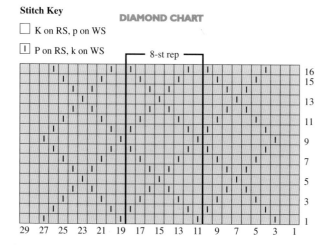

8-st rep

29 27 25 23 21 19 17 15 13 11 9 7 5 3 1

16 15 13 11 9 7 5 3 1

For Intermediate Knitters

Perfect for family game night, this intarsia-knit pullover with shapes and striped ribbing in bright colors makes a bold statement. Designed by Brandon Mably.

SIZES

Instructions are written for size 4. Changes for 6 are in parentheses.

KNITTED MEASUREMENTS

- Chest 27 (29)"/68.5 (73.5)cm
- Length 14½ (15½)"/37 (39)cm
- Upper arm 13 (14)"/33 (35.5)cm

MATERIALS

- 5 (6) 1¾oz/50g balls (each approx 92yd/84m) of Rowan Yarn *Handknit Cotton DK* (cotton ③) in #287 periwinkle (MC)
- 1 ball each in #202 turquoise (A), #229 yellow (B) and #219 lime (C)
- One pair each sizes 4 and 6 (3.5 and 4mm) needles or *size to obtain gauge*
- Bobbins
- Stitch holders
- Stitch markers

GAUGE

21 sts and 27 rows to 4"/10cm over St st foll chart using size 6 (4mm) needles. *Take time to check gauge.*

Notes I Do not carry yarns across. **2** Wind yarn onto bobbins. Work each motif with separate bobbins and use separate bobbins for background color. **3** When changing colors, twist yarn on WS to prevent holes in work.

STRIPED RIB

Work in k1, p1 rib and work 2 rows MC, 1 row A, 2 rows MC, 1 row B, 2 rows MC, 1 row C and 2 rows MC.

BACK

With smaller needles and MC, cast on 71 (77) sts. Work in striped rib, end with a WS row. Change to larger needles and cont in St st with MC. Work even for 10 (14) rows, end with a WS row. Work chart in chosen size through row 80 (82), end with a WS row.

Neck and shoulder shaping

Bind off 11 (12) sts at beg of next 2 rows, then 12 (13) sts at beg of next 2 rows. Place rem 25 (27) sts on a holder for back neck.

FRONT

Work as for back through row 44 (46).

Neck and shoulder shaping

Row 45 (47) Work first 35 (38) sts, place center st on a holder, join another ball of MC, work to end. Working both sides at once, dec 1 st at each neck edge every other row twice, every 3rd row 10 (11) times—23 (25) sts each side. Work to row 80 (82), end with a WS row. Shape shoulders as for back.

LEFT SLEEVE

With smaller needles and MC, cast on 37

(39) sts. Work in striped rib, inc 3 st evenly spaced across last row—40 (42) sts. Change to larger needles and cont with MC. **Next row (RS)** K12 (13), pm, k16, pm, k12 (13). Beg with a p row, cont in St st and inc 1 st each side every 4th row 14 (16) times, AT THE SAME TIME, when piece measures 4½ (5¼)"/11.5 (13)cm from beg, end with a WS row.

Beg chart pat

Row 1 (RS) Work to marker, work 16 sts of left sleeve chart, work to end. Cont as established to row 16; drop markers. When incs have been completed, work even on 68 (74) sts until piece measures 10 (11)"/25.5 (28)cm from beg, end with a WS row. Bind off.

RIGHT SLEEVE
Work as for left sleeve, foll chart for right sleeve.

FINISHING
Block pieces to measurements. Sew left shoulder seam.

Neckband

With RS facing, smaller needles and MC, k25 (27) back neck sts, pick up and k 30 (32) sts along left neck edge to center st, pm, k center st, pm, k30 (32) sts along right neck edge—86 (92) sts. **Next row (WS)** Work in k1, p1 rib to 2 sts before marker, dec 1 st , p1, dec 1 st, rib to end. Cont to dec 1 st each side of center marked k st and work in foll striped pat: 1 row C, 1 row MC, 1 row B and 1 row MC. With MC, bind off loosely in rib. Sew right shoulder/neckband seam. Place markers at 6½ (7)"/16.5 (17.5)cm down from shoulders. Sew sleeves to armholes between markers. Sew side and sleeve seams.

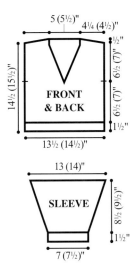

LEFT SLEEVE　　　**RIGHT SLEEVE**

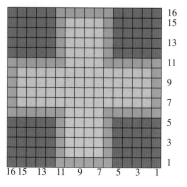 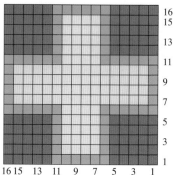

Color Key

- ■ Periwinkle (MC)
- ■ Turquoise (A)
- □ Yellow (B)
- ■ Lime (C)

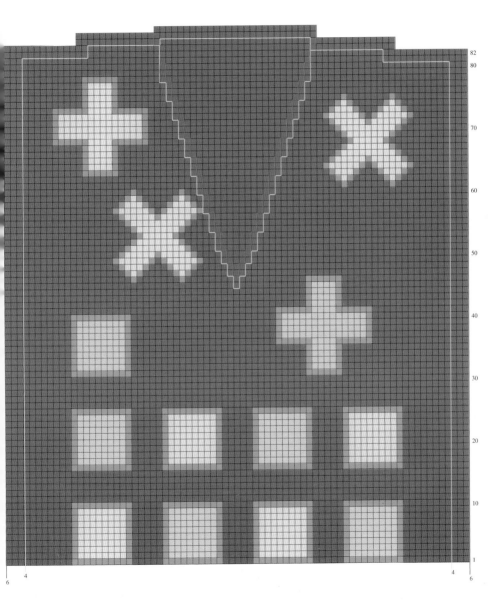

PURR-FECT CARDIGAN
The cat's meow

Designed by Jean Guirguis, this playful cardigan is sure to capture the attention of everyone. A simple drop-shoulder silhouette and stockinette stitch make the knitting easy, and the whimsical cut-out felt cat adds flair.

SIZES
Instructions are written for size 4. Changes for 6 and 8 are in parentheses.

KNITTED MEASUREMENTS
▪ Chest (buttoned) 26 (28, 31)"/66 (71, 78.5)cm
▪ Length 14 (15, 16)"/35.5 (38, 40.5)cm
▪ Upper arm 11 (12, 13)"/28 (30.5, 33)cm

MATERIALS
▪ 4 (5, 6) 1¾oz/50g skeins (each approx 138yd/126m) of Classic Elite Yarns *Waterspun* (wool④) in #5058 red (MC)
▪ 1 (1, 1) skein #5013 black (CC)
▪ One pair size 6 (4mm) needles *or size to obtain gauge*
▪ Stitch holder
▪ Five ⅝"/16mm buttons
▪ 8"/20cm square of black wool felt
▪ ½yd/.5m of ⅞"/22mm-wide ribbon
▪ Fabri-Tac fabric glue
▪ Black sewing thread

GAUGE
20 sts and 28 rows to 4"/10cm over St st using size 6 (4mm) needles.
Take time to check gauge.

BACK
With MC, cast on 65 (71, 77) sts. Work in k1, p1 rib for 3 rows, end with a RS row. Beg with a p row, cont in St st until piece measures 14 (15, 16)"/35.5 (38, 40.5)cm from beg.
Shoulder shaping
Bind off 18 (21, 23) sts at beg of next 2 rows. Place rem k 29 (29, 31) sts on a holder for back neck.

LEFT FRONT
With MC, cast on 31 (33, 37) sts. Work in k1, p1 rib for 3 rows, inc 0 (1, 0) st on last row—31 (34, 37) sts. Beg with a p row, cont in St st until piece measures 12 (13, 14)"/30.5 (33, 35.5)cm from beg, end with a RS row.
Neck shaping
Next row (WS) Bind off 5 (5, 6) sts (neck edge), work to end. Cont to shape neck, binding off 3 sts once, then 2 sts once. Dec 1 st from neck edge every other row 3 times—18 (21, 23) sts. Work even until same length as back. Bind off sts for shoulder.

RIGHT FRONT
Work to correspond to left front, reversing shaping.

SLEEVES
With MC, cast on 29 (31, 33) sts. Work in k1, p1 rib for 3 rows. Cont in St st, inc 1 st each side every 4th row 7 (10, 12) times,

then every 6th row 6 (5, 4) times—55 (61, 65) sts. Work even until piece measures 10½ (11½, 12½)"/ 26.5 (29, 31.5)cm from beg. Bind off.

Block pieces to measurements. Sew shoulder seams.

Buttonband

With RS facing and MC, pick up and k 69 (75, 81) sts evenly along left front edge. Work in k1, p1 rib for 3 rows. Bind off loosely in rib. Mark placement of 5 buttons on band, with first and last ½"/1.5cm from top and bottom edges and 3 spaced evenly between.

Buttonhole band

On right front, work as for buttonband until 1 row of rib is completed. **Buttonhole row** *Rib to marker, k2tog, yo; rep from * to end. Work in rib for 1 more row, then bind off loosely in rib.

Collar

With RS facing and MC, pick and k 65 (65, 67) sts evenly around neck edge excluding front bands. Work in k1, p1 rib for 2½ (3, 3½)"/6 (7.5, 9)cm. Bind off loosely in rib.

Cat motif

Cut cat from felt foll template. Glue cat to right front (see photo). Make a 2½"/6cm-wide bow with 2"/5cm-long streamers from ribbon. Make swallow tail cuts into end of each streamer. Sew bow to cat using thread.

Ball of yarn

Working from skein, wind CC into a flat, 1½"/4cm-diameter ball. Stitch with thread to secure winds, then sew ball to left front, as shown. Form free end of yarn into loops (pinning to secure in place), going up left front, down and up back, then down right front, over cat's paw, ending at bottom edge. On WS, sew yarn and loops in place using small blind-stitches. Sew side and sleeve seams. Sew on buttons.

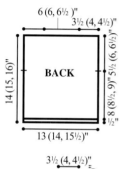

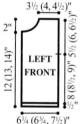

CAT TEMPLATE
ENLARGE 200%

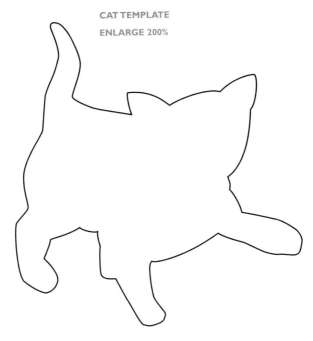

ANGORA WRAP CARDIGAN

Prima ballerina

For Intermediate Knitters

Your budding ballerina will love this pretty pink eyelet pattern surplice top. Folded under stockinette hems and I-cord ties add the finishing touches. Designed by Kaleigh Young.

SIZES

Instructions are written for size 4. Changes for 6, 8 and 10 are in parentheses.

KNITTED MEASUREMENTS

▪ Chest (closed) 26 (28, 31, 33)"/66 (71, 78.5, 84)cm

▪ Length 11½ (12½, 13½, 14½)"/29 (31.5, 34, 37)cm

▪ Upper arm 10 (11, 12, 13)"/25.5 (28, 30.5, 33)cm

MATERIALS

▪ 6 (6, 7, 8) ⅞oz/25g balls (each approx 116yd/106m) of Anny Blatt *Angora Super* (angora/wool③) in #164 pink

▪ One pair each sizes 4 and 6 (3.5 and 4 mm) *or size to obtain gauge*

▪ Size 4 (3.5mm) circular needle, 24"/60cm long

▪ One set (4) size 4 (3.5mm) dpn

GAUGE

22 sts and 30 rows to 4"/10cm over St st using size 6 (4mm) needles.
Take time to check gauge.

EYELET PATTERN STITCH
(multiple of 7 sts plus 1)

Rows 1 and 5 (RS) Knit.

Row 2 and all WS rows Purl.

Row 3 *K5, yo, k2tog; rep from *, end k1.

Row 7 K1, *yo, k2tog, k5; rep from * to end.

Row 8 Purl.

Rep rows 1-8 for eyelet pat st

BACK

With larger needles cast on 71 (78, 85, 92) sts. Work in eyelet pat st until piece measures 6½ (7, 7½, 8)"/16.5 (17.5, 19, 20)cm from beg, end with a WS row.

Armhole shaping

Bind off 4 sts at beg of next 2 rows. Dec 1 st each side every other row 3 times—57 (64, 71, 78) sts. Work even until armhole measures 5 (5½, 6, 6½)"/12.5 (14, 15, 16.5)cm, end with a WS row.

Neck shaping

Next row (RS) Work 17 (20, 23, 26) sts, join 2nd ball of yarn and bind off center 23 (24, 25, 26) sts for back neck, work to end. Working both sides at once, dec 1 st from each neck edge *every* row twice—15 (18, 21, 24) sts each side. Work even until armhole measures 5½ (6, 6½, 7)"/14 (15, 16.5, 17.5)cm. Bind off each side for shoulders.

LEFT FRONT

With larger needles cast on 71 (78, 85, 92) sts. Work in eyelet pat for 2 rows.

Neck and armhole shaping

Cont in pat and work neck decs as foll:

Row 1 (RS) Work to last 2 sts, k2tog.

Row 2 P2tog, work to end. **Row 3** Work even. **Row 4** P2tog, work to end. **Row 5** Work to last 2 sts, k2tog. **Row 6** Work even. Rep last 6 rows for neck decs until there are a total of 49 (53, 57, 61) neck decs, AT SAME TIME, when piece measures 6½ (7, 7½, 8)"/16.5 (17.5, 19, 20)cm beg, shape armhole at beg of RS rows as for back. When neck decs have been completed, work even on 15 (18, 21, 24) sts until same length as back. Bind off.

RIGHT FRONT

Work to correspond to left front, reversing shaping.

SLEEVES

With smaller needles cast on 38 (38, 45, 45) sts. Work in St st for 1"/2.5cm, dec 1 st each side on last row and end with a WS row—36 (36, 43, 43) sts. Change to larger needles. Work in eyelet pat st for 4 rows. Cont in pat, inc 1 st at each side (working incs into pat), every 6th row 10 (13, 12, 14) times—56 (62, 67, 71) sts. Work even until piece measures 11 (12, 13, 14)"/28 (30.5, 33, 35.5)cm from beg.

Cap shaping
Bind off 4 sts at beg of next 2 rows. Dec 1 st each side every other row 11 (14, 16, 18) times, then *every* row 10 times. Bind off rem 6 (6, 7, 7) sts.

FINISHING

Lightly block pieces to measurements.

I-cord ties
(make 4)
With dpn, cast on 4 sts. Work in I-cord as foll: ***Next row (RS)** With 2nd dpn, k4, do not turn. Slide sts back to beg of needle to work next row from RS; rep from * until I-cord measures 13 (13, 14, 15)"/33 (33, 35.5, 38)cm from beg. Cut yarn leaving a long tail. Thread tail into tapestry needle, then weave needle through sts; fasten off. Sew shoulder seams.

Neckband
With RS facing and circular needle, pick up and k 91 (98, 105, 112) sts along right front edge, 36 (37, 38, 39) sts along back

neck edge and 91 (98, 105, 112) sts along left front edge—218 (233, 248, 263) sts. Beg with a p row, work in St st for 1"/2.5cm. Bind off. Fold band in half to WS and sew in place. Sew sleeves into armholes. Side side seams, sewing a tie into seam ⅛"/.5cm from bottom edge. Sew sleeve seams. Turn bottom edge of each sleeve ½"/1.5cm to WS and sew in place.

Bottom band

With RS facing and circular needle, pick up and k 76 (83, 90, 97) sts evenly spaced along left front to first side seam, then 68 (75, 82, 89) sts along back to within ½"/1.5cm of next side seam. Cast on 5 sts (eyelet opening), then beg ½"/1.5cm from side seam, pick up and k 74 (81, 88, 95) sts along right front—223 (244, 265, 286) sts. Beg with a p row, work in St st for 1"/2.5cm. Bind off. Fold band in half to WS, then sew in place, sewing cast-on edge of eyelet opening to bound-off edge of band. Sew rem ties to beg of neck shaping on left and right front edges.

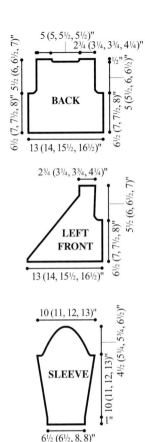

Very Easy Very Vogue

This basic silhouette designed by Kirstin Spurkland is sure to please boys and girls alike. A textural rib pattern and dark color for the sleeves is a cool contrast to the stockinette stitch, lighter color body. A color block rectangle on the front adds a bit of fun.

SIZES

Instructions are written for size 4. Changes for 6, 8 and 10 are in parentheses.

KNITTED MEASUREMENTS

▪ Chest 29 (30, 32, 34)"/73.5 (76, 81, 86)cm
▪ Length 15 (16, 17, 18)"/38 (40.5, 43, 45.5)cm
▪ Upper arm 12½ (13½, 14½, 15½)"/31.5 (34, 37, 39)cm

MATERIALS

▪ 5 (6, 6, 7) 1¾oz/50g skeins (each approx 63yd/58m) of GGH/Muench *Aspen* (wool/microfiber⑤) in #26 green (MC)
▪ 4 (4, 5, 5) skeins in #7 brown (CC)
▪ One pair each sizes 10 and 10½ (6 and 6.5mm) needles *or size to obtain gauge*
▪ One set (4) size 10½ (6.5mm) dpn
▪ Size 10 (6 mm) circular needle, 16"/40cm long
▪ Stitch holders

GAUGES

▪ 13 sts and 18 rows to 4"/10cm over St st using size 10½ (6.5mm) needles.

▪ 14 sts and 20 rows to 4"/10cm over rib pat using size 10½ (6.5mm) needles.
Take time to check gauges.

Note When changing colors, twist yarn on WS to prevent holes in work.

RIB PATTERN

(multiple of 3 sts)
Row 1 (RS) K1, *k2, p1; rep from * end k2.
Row 2 P2, *k2, p1; rep from * end p1.
Rep rows 1 and 2 for rib pat.

BACK

With smaller straight needles and MC, cast on 48 (51, 54, 57) sts. Work in rib pat for 8 rows. **Next row (RS)** Knit, dec 1 (2, 2, 1) sts evenly spaced across—47 (49, 52, 56) sts. P 1 row. Cont in St st until piece measures 15 (16, 17, 18)"/38 (40.5, 43, 45.5)cm from beg, end with a WS row.
Neck and shoulder shaping
Next row (RS) K 14 (15, 16, 17) sts and place on a holder, k 19 (19, 20, 22) sts for back neck and place on a holder, k rem 14 (15, 16, 17) sts and place on a holder.

FRONT

Work as for back until piece measures 8 (9, 9, 10)"/20 (23, 23, 25.5)cm from beg, end with a WS row.
Color block
Row 1 (RS) K 10 (11, 12, 13) with MC, k 27 (27, 28, 30) with CC, k 10 (11, 12, 13) with MC. **Row 2** P 10 (11, 12, 13) with

MC, p 27 (27, 28, 30) with CC, p 10 (11, 12, 13) with MC. Rep these 2 rows 6 (6, 7, 7) times more. With MC only, work even until piece measures 12½ (13½, 14½, 15½)"/31.5 (34, 37, 39)cm from beg, end with a WS row.

Neck shaping

Next row (RS) Work 19 (20, 21, 22) sts, with separate skein of MC, work 9 (9, 10, 12) sts for front neck and place on a holder, work to end. Working both sides at once, bind off 2 sts from each neck edge once, dec 1 st at each neck edge every other row 3 times. Work even until same length as back. Place 14 (15, 16, 17) sts each side on holders for shoulders.

SLEEVES

With smaller straight needles and CC, cast on 24 (24, 27, 27) sts. Work in rib pat for 8 rows. Change to larger needles and cont in rib pat, inc 1 st each side (working incs into pat), every 4th row 5 (9, 6, 8) times, then every 6th row 5 (3, 6, 6) times—44 (48, 51, 55) sts. Work even until piece measures 12 (13, 14, 15)"/30.5 (33, 35.5, 38)cm from beg. Bind off.

FINISHING

Block pieces to measurements. Join first shoulder tog as folls: With RS of pieces tog, sl shoulder sts to 2 dpn. With 3rd dpn, and shoulder sts parallel, k 1st from back dpn with 1 st from front dpn and bind off while working tog for three-needle bind off. Rep for rem shoulder.

Neckband

With RS facing, circular needle and MC, pick up and k 42 (42, 45, 48) sts evenly around neck. Join and work in foll rib pat: **Rnd 1** *K2, p1; rep from *. **Rnd 2** *K1, p2; rep from *. Rep these 2 rnds for 1"/2.5cm. Bind off loosely in rib pat. Place markers at 6¼ (6¾, 7¼, 7¾)"/16 (17, 18.5, 19.5)cm down from shoulders. Sew sleeves to armholes between markers. Sew side and sleeve seams.

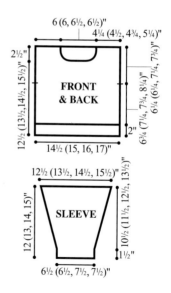

Patriot games

Keep your little tyke warm in this stars and stripes set. Both are made circularly so that there are no bulky seams and the star motifs are knit-in. Designed by Lipp Holmfeld.

SIZES

Instructions are written for size 4-6. Changes for 8-10 are in parentheses.

KNITTED MEASUREMENTS

- Head circumference 16 (17½)"/40.5 (44.5)cm
- Hand width 3¼ (3¼)"/8 (8)cm
- Hand length 6¾ (7½)"/17 (19)cm

MATERIALS

- 1 3½oz/100g balls (each approx 110yd/ 101m) of Lane Borgosesia *Knitusa*® (wool④) each in #3792 red (A), #95005 white (B) and #176 blue (C)
- Size 8 (5mm) circular needle, 16"/40cm long, *or size to obtain gauge*
- One set (4) size 8 (5mm) dpn
- Bobbin
- Stitch marker

GAUGE

17 sts and 22 rows to 4"/10cm over St st using size 8 (5mm) needles.
Take time to check gauge.

Notes 1 Wind only B onto bobbin. **2** As you work in the round, carry C across WS of star motif, stranding floats. **3** On WS, bring B back to the right to work next chart row, also stranding floats. **4** When changing colors, twist yarn on WS to prevent holes in work.

HAT

With circular needle and A, cast on 76 (84) sts. Join and pm for beg of rnds. Work in k1, p1 rib for 15 rnds. Change to B and St st. **Next (dec) rnd** [K2, k2tog] 19 (21) times—57 (63) sts. Work for 7 (8) more rnds. Change to C and work for 3 (5) rnds.

Beg chart pat

Next rnd K 24 (27) with C, beg pat at st 3 and work to st 11, k to end with C. Work chart to row 13, then cont to work with C only for 3 (4) rnds. Change to dpns and divide sts evenly between 3 needles.

Crown shaping

Rnd 1 *K17 (19), p2tog; rep from * around—54 (60) sts. **Rnd 2** *K17 (19), p1; rep from * around. **Rnd 3** *K7 (8), p2tog; rep from * around—48 (54) sts. **Rnd 4** *K7 (8), p1; rep from * around. **Rnd 5** *K6 (7), p2tog; rep from * around—42 (48) sts. **Rnd 6** *K6 (7), p1; rep from * around. **Rnd 7** *K5 (6), p2tog; rep from * around—36 (42) sts. **Rnd 8** *K5 (6), p1; rep from * around. **Rnd 9** *K4 (5), p2tog; rep from * around—30 (36) sts. **Rnd 10** *K4 (5), p1; rep from * around. **Rnd 11** *K3 (4), p2tog; rep from * around—24 (30) sts. **Rnd 12** *K3 (4), p1; rep from * around. **Rnd 13** *K2 (3), p2tog; rep from * around—18 (24) sts. For size 8-10 only [K2, p2tog] 6 times—18 sts. Cut yarn leaving a long tail. Thread tail into tapestry needle and weave through sts. Pull tight to gather, fasten off securely.

Block lightly.
Pompom
With A and B, make a pompom 3"/7.5cm in diameter. Sew pompom to top of hat.

With dpn and A, cast on 26 sts. Divide sts between 3 dpn as foll: 13 sts on 1st dpn, 6 sts on 2nd dpn and 7 sts on 3rd dpn. Join and pm for beg of rnds.
Cuff
Work in k1, p1 rib for 5 rnds. Change to B and cont in rib for 4 rnds. **Next rnd** Work in rib to last 2 sts, k2tog—25 sts. Change to C and St st.
Hand
Work even for 5 (7) rnds.
Beg chart pat
Row 1 Beg pat at st 1 and work to st 13, then work to end. Work chart to row 12. AT THE SAME TIME, work until 4 rnds have been completed.
Thumb positioning
Next rnd Work to within last 4 sts of rnd. K these 4 sts with a separate strand of B, then place these sts back to LH dpn and k again with C yarn in progress. When chart is completed, cont to work with C only for 3 (5) rnds.

Top shaping
Dec rnd 1 [SKP, k9, k2tog] twice—22 sts. **Next rnd** Knit. **Dec rnd 2** [SKP, k7, k2tog] twice—18 sts. **Next rnd** Knit. **Dec rnd 3** [SKP, k5, k2tog] twice—14 sts. **Dec rnd 4** [K2tog] 7 times—7sts. Cut yarn leaving a long tail. Thread tail into tapestry needle and weave through sts. Pull tight to gather, fasten off securely.
Thumb
Carefully remove contrast yarn and place 4 sts on 1st dpn and 4 sts on 2nd dpn. **Next (inc) rnd** K4, M1, k4, M1—10 sts. Work even for 5 (7) rnds. **Next (dec) rnd** [K2tog] 5 times—5 sts. Cut yarn leaving a long tail. Thread tail into tapestry needle and weave through sts. Pull tight to gather, fasten off securely.

Work as for left mitten to thumb positioning.
Thumb positioning
Next rnd Work first 13 sts. K next 4 sts with a separate strand of B, then place these sts back to LH dpn and k again with C yarn in progress, work to end. Cont to work as for left mitten.

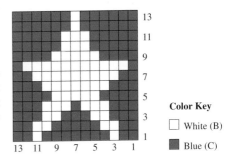

Color Key
☐ White (B)
■ Blue (C)

For Intermediate Knitters

Colorful garter-stitch stripes make up the body of Irina Poludnenko's zippered cardigan and the crown on the cap. The cardigan is knit in one piece to the armhole. The bands at the lower edges are knit horizontally then sewn on, and crocheted bobbles adorn the edges.

SIZES

Cardigan instructions are written for size 4. Changes for 6, 8 and 10 are in parentheses. Hat instructions are written for sizes 4-6. Changes for 8-10 are in parentheses.

KNITTED MEASUREMENTS

Cardigan
- Chest (closed) 30 (32, 34, 36)"/76 (81, 86, 91.5)cm
- Length 15 (16, 17, 18)"/38 (40.5, 43, 45.5)cm
- Upper arm 13 (14, 15, 16)"/33 (35.5, 38, 40.5)cm

Hat
- Head circumference measures 16¼ (17½)"/41 (44.5)cm

MATERIALS

- 4 (5, 5, 6) 1¾oz/50g skeins (each approx 137yd/125m) of Plymouth Yarns *Wildfower D.K.* (cotton/acrylic③) in #56 pink (A)
- 2 skeins each in #51 white (B), #54 orange (C) and #63 red (D)
- One pair size 6 (4mm) needles *or size to obtain gauge*

- Size 6 (4mm) circular needle, 24"/60cm long
- Size G/6 (4mm) crochet hook
- Stitch holder
- One 15 (16, 17, 18)"/38 (40.5, 43, 45.5)cm separating white zipper

GAUGE

22 sts and 40 rows to 4"/10cm over garter st using size 6 (4mm) needles.
Take time to check gauge.

Notes 1 Bottom band, neckband and hat-band are made vertically. **2** Body is worked in one piece to armhole, then both fronts and back are worked separately to shoulder.

RIDGE PATTERN

Rows 1, 3 and 5 (RS) Purl.
Rows 2 and 4 Knit.
Rows 6 and 8 Purl.
Rows 7 and 9 Knit.
Row 10 Purl.
Rep rows 1-10 for ridge pat.

STRIPE PATTERN

Work 2 rows each of A, C, A, D, A and B. Rep these 12 rows for stripe pat.

BODY

Bottom band
With straight needles and A, cast on 14 (14, 18, 18) sts. Work in ridge pat until piece measures approx 26½ (28, 30, 32½)"/67 (71, 76, 82.5)cm from beg, end

with row 5. Bind off. With RS facing, circular needle and B, pick up and k 164 (176, 188, 198) sts evenly spaced along entire bottom band. **Next row (WS)** Knit. Working in garter st, work even in stripe pat until piece measures 8½ (9, 9½, 10)"/21.5 (23, 24, 25.5)cm from bottom edge of band, end with a WS row.

Separate for fronts and back

Next row (RS) Work 38 (41, 44, 46) sts and place on holder for right front, bind off 6 (6, 6, 7) sts, work until there are 76 (82, 88, 92) sts for back, leave rem sts unworked for left front. Change to straight needles and cont to work back sts only until armhole measures 6½ (7, 7½, 8)"/16.5 (17.5, 19, 20)cm.

Neck and shoulder shaping

Bind off 8 (9, 9, 10) sts at beg of next 4 rows, 8 (8, 10, 10) sts at beg of next 2 rows. Bind off rem 28 (30, 32, 32) sts for back neck.

Return to 38 (41, 44, 46) sts on right front and work even until armhole measures 4½ (5, 5½, 6)"/11.5 (12.5, 14, 15)cm, end with a WS row.

Neck and shoulder shaping

Next row (RS) Bind off 4 sts (neck edge), work to end. Cont to bind off from neck edge 3 sts once, 2 sts once, dec 1 st *every* row 5 (6, 7, 7) times—24 (26, 28, 30) sts. When armhole measures 6½ (7, 7½,

8)"/16.5 (17.5, 19, 20)cm, shape shoulder at beg of WS rows as for back.

Join MC to rem sts and bind off 6 (6, 6, 7) sts for armhole. Complete as for right front reversing shaping.

With straight needles and A, cast on 38 (38, 40, 42) sts. Work in garter st for 2 rows. Beg with a B stripe, cont in stripe pat, inc 1 st each side every 4th row 4 (6, 6, 7), every 6th row 13 (14, 15, 16) times—72 (78, 82, 88) sts. Work even until piece measures 11(12, 13, 14)"/28 (30.5, 33, 35.5)cm from beg. Bind off.

Block pieces to measurements. Sew shoulder seams.

Neckband

With straight needles and A, cast on 10 sts. Beg with row 1 (3, 1, 1), work in rib pat until piece measures 15½ (16, 16½, 16½)"/39 (40.5, 42, 42)cm from beg, end with row 5 (3, 5, 5). Bind off. Sew neckband to neck edge.

Front edging

With RS facing, crochet hook and A, work a row of sc evenly along front edge. Fasten off. Rep on other front. Sew in zipper. Sew sleeves into armholes, beg and end at center of bound-off sts. Sew sleeve seams.

Bobbles

On WS, make a bobble in each St st section of rib bands. Alternate colors B, C and D, as shown. To make a bobble, first make a lp and place on hook. With WS facing, insert hook 2 sts down from edge and centered side to side. Yo and draw up a lp. Yo and draw through 1 lp on hook, then yo and draw through 2 lps on hook (first dc made); make 4 more dc in same sp. Fasten off. Draw in loose ends.

HAT

Hatband

With straight needles and A, cast on 18 sts. Work in rib pat until piece measures 16¼ (17½)"/41 (44.5)cm from beg. Bind off.

With RS facing and A, pick up and k 92 (104) sts evenly spaced along entire hatband. **Next row (WS)** Knit. Working in garter st, work even in stripe pat for 22 (26) rows. **Next row (RS)** K1, [pm, k 15 (16)] 6 times, end k1. **Next row** Knit. **Dec row (RS)** K1, [sl marker, k2tog, k to next marker] 6 times, end k1—86 (98) sts. **Next row** Knit. Rep last 2 rows until 8 sts rem. Cut yarn leaving a long tail. Thread tail into tapestry needle and weave through sts. Pull tight to gather, fasten off securely.

FINISHING

Sew back seam.

Bobbles

Work as for cardigan.

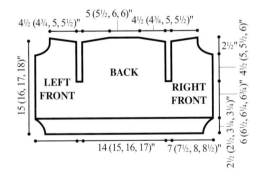

Use these two basic colors or have the child pick their favorite shades to make this simple hooded pullover, accented with a shaped patch pocket and zippered placket. Designed by Bonnie Franz.

SIZES

Instructions are written for size 4. Changes for 6, 8 and 10 are in parentheses.

KNITTED MEASUREMENTS

- Chest 31 (32, 34, 36)"/78.5 (81, 86, 91.5)cm
- Length (with edge rolled) 13½ (14½, 15½, 16½)"/34 (37, 39, 42)cm
- Upper arm 14 (15, 16, 17)"/35.5 (38, 40.5, 43)cm

MATERIALS

- 2 8¾oz/250g hanks (each approx 310yd/ 283m) of Wool Pak Yarns NZ/Baabajoes Wool Co. *14 Ply* (wool⑤) in #14 navy (MC)
- 1 hank in #30 green (CC)
- One pair size 10 (6mm) needles *or size to obtain gauge*
- One size 9 (5.5mm) dpn
- One 5"/125mm navy neck zipper

GAUGE

14 sts and 19 rows to 4"/10cm over St st using size 10 (6mm) needles.
Take time to check gauge.

BACK

With MC, cast on 54 (56, 60, 64) sts.

Work in St st for 14½ (15½, 16½, 17½)"/37 (39, 42, 44.5)cm.

Back neck and shoulder shaping
Bind off 16 (17, 18, 20) sts at beg of next 2 rows. Bind off rem 22 (22, 24, 24) sts for back neck.

FRONT

Work as for back until piece measures 7½ (8½, 9½, 10½)"/19 (21.5, 24, 26.5)cm from beg, end with a WS row.

Neck opening
Next row (RS) Work 26 (27, 29, 31) sts, join another hank of MC and bind off 2 sts, work to end. Working both sides at once, cast on 2 sts (facings) at each neck opening once—28 (29, 31, 33) sts each side. Work even until neck opening measures 5"/12.5cm from beg, end with a WS row.

Neck shaping
Bind off 7 (7, 8, 8) sts from each neck once, dec 1 st *every* row 5 times—16 (17, 18, 20) sts each side. Work even until piece measures same as back. Bind off sts each side.

Pocket
Count 10 (10, 12, 14) rows up from lower edge, then count 12 (13, 14, 16) sts from right side edge. With RS facing and CC, pick up and k 30 (30, 32, 32) sts working each pick-up st into strand behind each of center 30 (30, 32, 32) sts on front; take care that all sts are picked up across the same row. Beg with a p row, work in St st for 5 (7, 9, 9) rows, end with a WS row. Dec 1 st each side every other row 8 times—14 (14, 16, 16) sts. Do not bind off.

Bind off and join pocket

On front, count 22 (24, 26, 26) rows up from lower edge of pocket, then count 20 (21, 22, 24) sts from right side edge. With dpn and working into strand behind each st, pick up 14 (14, 16, 16) center sts on front. Place pocket needle parallel with front sts on dpn. To bind off and join, k 1 st of pocket tog with 1 st of front needle.

SLEEVES

With CC, cast on 32 (33, 34, 36) sts. Work even in St st for 8 rows, end with a WS row. Inc 1 st each side every 4th row 4 (5, 5, 6) times, every 6th row 5 (5, 6, 6) times—50 (53, 56, 60) sts. Work even until piece measures 12 (13, 14, 15)"/30.5 (33, 35.5, 38)cm from beg. Bind off.

FINISHING

Block pieces lightly to measurements, allowing lower edges of pieces to roll as in photo. Sew straight side edges of pocket in place. Fold front neck facings to WS and baste in place. Sew in zipper under neck opening; remove basting sts. Sew shoulder seams.

HOOD

With RS facing and MC, pick up and k 50 (50, 54, 54) sts evenly along neck. Beg with a p row, cont in St st for 3 rows, end with a WS row.

Hood shaping

Inc row 1 (RS) K24 (24, 26, 26), M1, k2, M1, k24 (24, 26, 26)—52 (52, 56, 56) sts. Work 3 rows even. **Inc row 2 (RS)** K25 (25, 27, 27), M1, k2, M1, k25 (25, 27, 27)—54 (54, 58, 58) sts. Work 3 rows even. **Inc row 3** K26 (26, 28, 28), M1, k2, M1, k26 (26, 28, 28)—56 (56, 60, 60) sts. Work 3 rows even. **Inc row 4** K27 (27, 29, 29), M1, k2, M1, k27 (27, 29, 29)—58 (58, 62, 62) sts. Work 5 rows even. **Inc row 5** K28 (28, 30, 30), M1, k2, M1, k28 (28, 30, 30)—60 (60, 64, 64) sts. Work even until hood measures 10 (10½, 11, 12)"/25.5 (26.5, 28, 30.5)cm from beg. Bind off. Sew top of hood seam.

Hood edging

With RS facing and MC, pick up and k 72 (76, 80, 86) sts evenly along front edge. Cont in St st for 5 rows. Bind off loosely. Place markers at 7 (7½, 8, 8½)"/17.5 (19, 20, 21.5)cm down from shoulders. Sew sleeves to armholes between markers. Sew side and sleeve seams.

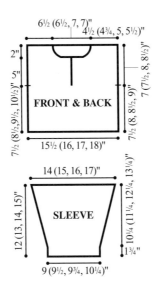

6½ (6½, 7, 7)"
4½ (4¾, 5, 5½)"

2"

5"

7 (7½, 8, 8½)"

FRONT & BACK

7½ (8½, 9½, 10½)"

7½ (8, 8½, 9)"

15½ (16, 17, 18)"

14 (15, 16, 17)"

10¼ (11¼, 12¼, 13¼)"

SLEEVE

12 (13, 14, 15)"

1¾"

9 (9½, 9¾, 10¼)"

Basic garter stitch, colorful fringed edges and I-cord make this a great project for beginner knitters. Make a matching striped purse for those girly essentials. Designed by Carol Gillis.

SIZES

Instructions are written for size 4. Changes for 6, 8 and 10 are in parentheses.

KNITTED MEASUREMENTS

Pullover

Chest 25 (26, 29, 31)"/63.5 (66, 73.5, 78.5)cm

Length 12½ (13½, 14½, 15½)"/31.5 (34, 37, 39)cm

Upper arm 12 (13, 14, 15)"/30.5 (33, 35.5, 38)cm

Purse

5½" x 5½"/14 x 14cm

MATERIALS

6 (7, 7, 8) 1¾oz/50g balls (each approx 84yd/77m) of Mission Falls/Unique Kolours *1824 Cotton* (cotton④) in #404 indigo (MC)

1 ball each in #203 cosmos (A), #204 lentil (B), #302 wintergreen (C), #303 jade (D), #403 sky (E) and #406 lilac (F)

One pair size 7 (4.5mm) needles *or size to obtain gauge*

One set (4) size 7 (4.5mm) dpn

Size H/8 (5mm) crochet hook

Stitch holders

GAUGE

18 sts and 30 rows to 4"/10cm over garter st using size 7 (4.5mm) needles.

Take time to check gauge.

PULLOVER

BACK

With MC, cast on 56 (60, 66, 70) sts. Work in garter st for 11½ (12½, 13½, 14½)"/29 (31.5, 34, 37)cm.

Neck shaping

Next row (RS) Work 18 (20, 22, 24) sts, join another ball of MC and bind off center 20 (20, 22, 22) sts for back neck, work to end. Working both side at once, dec 1 st at each neck edge every other row 3 times—15 (17, 19, 21) sts each side. Work even until piece measures 12½ (13½, 14½, 15½)"/31.5 (34, 37, 39)cm from beg. Bind off sts side for shoulders.

FRONT

Work as for back until piece measures 10 (11, 12, 13)"/25.5 (28, 30.5, 33)cm from beg, end with a WS row.

Neck shaping

Next row (RS) Work 21 (23, 25, 27) sts, join another ball of MC and bind off center 14 (14, 16, 16) sts for front neck, work to end. Working both side at once, dec 1 st at each neck edge every other row 6 times—15 (17, 19, 21) sts each side. Work even until piece measures same as back. Bind off each side.

SLEEVES

With MC, cast on 32 (32, 34, 36)) sts. Work in garter st, inc 1 st each side every 6th row 5 (6, 7, 7) times, every 4th row 7 (8, 8, 9) times—56 (60, 64, 68) sts. Work even until piece measures 8 (9, 10, 11)"/20 (23, 25.5, 28)cm from beg. Bind off.

FINISHING

Block pieces to measurements. Sew shoulder seams. Place markers at 6 (6½, 7, 7½)"/15 (16.5, 17.5, 19)cm down from shoulders. Sew sleeves to armholes between markers. Sew side and sleeve seams.

I-cord neck edging

With A and dpn, cast on 4 sts. Work in I-cord as foll: ***Next row (RS)** With 2nd dpn, k4, do *not* turn. Slide sts back to beg of needle to work next row from RS; rep from * for 6 more rows. Join B and work for 7 rows. Cont in this way working 7 rows each in C, D, E, F, A and B until cord measures 18 (18, 19, 19)"/45.5 (45.5, 48, 48)cm, or long enough to fit aound neck. Cut yarn leaving a long tail. Thread tail into tapestry needle, then weave needle through sts. Sew this end to opposite end forming a ring. Sew I-cord around neck edge, so joined ends are at center back neck.

Fringe

For each fringe, cut 4 strands 8"/20cm long. Use crochet hook to pull through and knot fringe. Knot fringe every 1"/2.5cm around lower edges of body and sleeves. See photo for color placement. Trim fringe to measure 2"/5cm long.

PURSE

Beg at top edge with MC, cast on 20 sts. Working in garter st, work for 4 rows.

Stripe pat 1

*Work 2 rows each in A, B, C, D, E and F; rep from * 3 times. With MC, work for 6 rows, end with a WS row.

Stripe pat 2

*Work 2 rows each in F, E, D, C, B and A; rep from * 3 times. With MC, work for 4 rows. Bind off for opposite top edge.

Side edging

With RS facing and MC, pick up and k 42 sts evenly spaced along first side edge. **Next row (WS)** K. Place 21 sts on each of

2 holders. Cut yarn leaving a 54"/137cm tail. Rep on 2nd side edge, but placing 21 sts on each of 2 dpn. Do *not* cut yarn.

Join side seams

Join first side seam tog as folls: Place RS tog. With 3rd dpn, and side edging sts parallel, k 1st from back dpn with 1 st from front dpn and bind off while working tog for three-needle bind off. Rep for 2nd seam.

I-cord strap

With MC and dpn, cast on 4 sts. Make I-cord as for pullover for 7 rows. Cont in stripe pat until I-cord measures approx 25 (26, 27½, 29)"/63.5 (66, 70, 73.5)cm, ending with 7 rows MC. Cut yarn leaving a long tail. Thread tail into tapestry needle, then weave needle through sts; fasten off. On inside of purse, sew each MC end to a side seam.

Fringe

Work as for pullover, knotting 7 fringe evenly spaced across bottom edge of purse. See photo for color placement.

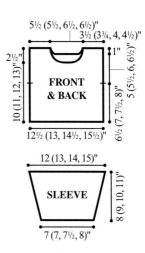

5½ (5½, 6½, 6½)"
3½ (3¾, 4, 4½)"
2½"
1"
10 (11, 12, 13)"
FRONT & BACK
6½ (7, 7½, 8)"
5 (5½, 6, 6½)"
12½ (13, 14½, 15½)"

12 (13, 14, 15)"
SLEEVE
8 (9, 10, 11)"
7 (7, 7½, 8)"

A reverse stockinette stitch knit firmly in a bulky wool gives the appearance of Austrian boiled wool, typical in Tyrolean jackets. Finished with faux pockets and an easy crochet edging and designed by Mari Lynn Patrick.

SIZES

Instructions are written for size 4. Changes for sizes 6 and 8 are in parentheses.

KNITTED MEASUREMENTS

Chest (buttoned) 33 (35, 37)"/84 (89, 94)cm

Length 16 (16¾, 18¾)"/40.5 (42.5, 47.5)cm

Upper arm 12½ (13, 13½)"/32 (33, 34)cm

MATERIALS

4 8oz/226g skeins (each approx 132yd/121m) of Brown Sheep Co. *Burly Spun* (wool ⑥) in #BS03 grey (MC)

1 skein in #BS181 rust (CC)

One pair size 13 (9mm) needles *or size to obtain gauge*

Size K/10½ (8mm) crochet hook

Five ⅞"/22mm buttons

GAUGE

10 sts and 13 rows to 4"/10cm over reverse St st using size 13 (9mm) needles. *Take time to check gauge.*

BACK

With size 13 (9mm) needles and MC, cast on 38 (41, 44) sts. Beg with a k (WS) row, work in reverse St st for 8 (8½, 10)"/20.5 (21.5, 25.5)cm.

Armhole shaping

Bind off 2 sts at beg of next 2 rows. Dec 1 st each side every other row 3 (4, 5) times—28 (29,30) sts. Work even until armhole measures 6¼ (6½, 7)"/16 (16.5, 18)cm.

Neck and shoulder shaping

Bind off 3 sts at beg of next 4 rows, 2 sts at beg of next 2 rows. Bind off center 12 (13, 14) sts for back neck.

LEFT FRONT

With size 13 (9mm) needles and MC, cast on 21 (23, 25) sts. Beg with a k (WS) row, work in reverse St st for 3½ (4, 4½)"/9 (10, 11.5)cm.

Pocket opening

Next row (RS) P6 (7, 9), bind off 10 sts, p to end. **Next row** Knit, casting on 10 sts over bound-off sts. Cont in reverse St st until piece measures 7½ (8, 9)"/19 (20.5, 23)cm from beg.

Beg lapel

Next row (RS) P to last 2 sts, inc 1 p st in next st, k1. Cont to inc 1 st in 2nd to the last st every 6th row twice more, AT SAME TIME, displace sts from purl to knit every other row 9 times more (that is, work 1 more st in knit and 1 less st in purl every RS row until there are 12 knit sts at lapel edge) AND work armhole shaping at side edge when same length as back—19 (20, 21) sts after all shaping is complete. Work even, if necessary, until lapel edge measures 5¾ (5¾, 6¼)"/14.5 (14.5, 16)cm, end with a RS row.

Lapel shaping

Next row (WS) Bind off 4 (4, 5) sts, k to end. Cont to shape at lapel edge binding off 4 sts once, 3 (4, 4) sts once. When same length as back, bind off 3 sts from shoulder edge twice, 2 sts once.

Work to correspond to left front, reversing shaping and pocket placements.

With size 13 (9mm) needles and MC, cast on 19 (20, 22) sts. Beg with a k (WS) row, work in reverse St st, inc 1 st each side every alternate 4th and 6th row a total of 6 times—31 (32, 34) sts. Work even until piece measures 10 (11, 12)"/25.5 (28, 30.5)cm from beg.

Cap shaping

Bind off 2 sts at beg of next 6 rows. Dec 1 st each side of next row then every other row twice more—13 (14, 16) sts. Bind off.

Block pieces to measurements. Sew shoulder seams.

Working on WS of jacket, beg at 8 sts from outside left lapel edge and ending at same st on right lapel edge, with size 13 (9mm) needles and MC, pick up and k 26 (30, 34) sts evenly around neck edge. K 1 row, p 1 row. **Next row (WS)** K7 (8, 10), M1, k4 (5, 5), M1, k4, M1, k4 (5, 5), M1, k7 (8, 10)—30 (34, 38) sts. Bind off 1 st at beg of next 4 rows. Work 3 rows even. Bind off rem 26 (30, 34) sts.

Pocket trims

With crochet hook and CC, sl st in each st of pocket opening. Ch 1, turn. **Next row (WS)** Sl st in front lps only of each sl st. Fasten off. Sew pocket openings closed.

Sleeve trim

With crochet hook and CC, sl st in each st of sleeve cuff. Ch 2, turn. **Next row (WS)** Work hdc in front lps only of each sl st. Fasten off. Set in sleeves. Sew side and sleeve seams.

Front and lower trims

Beg and end at beg of lapels, work as for sleeve trim, working from RS and working sl st, ch 1 and sl st in each lower corner on first row. On hdc row, work hdc, ch 1 and hdc in each corner and work 3 buttonholes as foll: (right front for girls, left front for boys) from top edge working 1 hdc, *ch 1, skip 1 st (buttonhole), hdc in next 4 sts; rep from * once, work 1 buttonhole, complete row.

Lapel trim

Working from RS (purl side) of lapel, beg and end at top of front bands, work sl st in each st around lapel and collar edges. Ch 1, turn. **Next row (WS)** *Sl st in each st of row through front loops only, to 1 st before inside lapel/collar joining, pull up a lp in next 3 sts, yo and through 3 lps on hook; rep from * once, work sl st to end. Sew on buttons opposite buttonholes. Locate corner of lapels on jacket fronts. Sew on button and pull through lapel jacket to close.

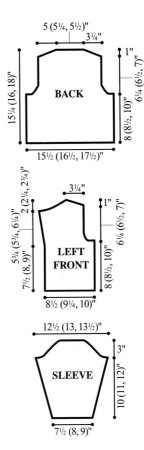

Very Easy Very Vogue

This easy poncho is knit in one piece, with openings at the lower body for little hands. Add a hood to keep head warm and cozy. Designed by Norah Gaughan.

SIZES

Instructions are written for size 6-8. Changes for 10 are in parentheses.

KNITTED MEASUREMENTS
■ Width around lower edge 48 (53)"/122 (134.5)cm
■ Length 18 (20½)"/45.5 (52)cm

MATERIALS
■ 6 (8) 3½oz/100g skeins (each approx 76yd/69m) of Artful Yarns/JCA *Museum* (wool⑥) in #4 orange
■ One each sizes 10½ and 11 (6.5 and 8mm) circular needle, 24"/60cm long, *or size to obtain gauge*
■ Size 11 (8mm) circular needle, 16"/40cm long
■ One set (4) size 10½ (6.5mm) dpn
■ Stitch marker

GAUGE
10 sts and 14 rows to 4"/10cm over St st using size 11 (8mm) needle.
Take time to check gauge.

BODY
With smaller circular needle, cast on 120 (132) sts. Join and pm for beg of rnds. Work in k1, p1 rib for 2 rnds. Change to size 11 (8mm) longer circular needle. Work in St st until piece measures 3 (4)"/7.5 (10)cm from beg.

Divide for hand slits
Next rnd Work 40 (44) sts, join another skein of yarn and work to end. **Next row** Work 20 (22) sts, turn. Work back and forth in St st using separate skeins of yarn for 5 (5½)"/12.5 (14)cm, end with a WS row. **Next (joining) rnd** K around, dropping 2nd skein of yarn. Work even until piece measures 10 (12½)"/25.5 (31.5)cm from beg.

Upper body shaping
Dec rnd 1 [K5, k2tog] 17 (18) times, end k 1(6)—103 (114) sts. Work even for 8 rnds. **Dec rnd 2** [K3, k2tog] 20 (22) times, end k 3 (4)—83 (92)sts. Change to shorter needle. Work even for 5 rnds. **Dec rnd 3** [K2, k2tog] 20 (22) times, end k 1(2), k2tog—62 (69)sts. Work even for 5 rnds. **Dec rnd 4** [K1, k2tog] 20 (23) times, end k 2 (0)—42 (46)sts.

Neck opening and shaping
Work back and forth in rows. **Next row** K 11(12), turn, p to end. **Dec row (RS)** K1, ssk, work to last 3 sts, k2tog, k1. **Next row** Purl. Rep last 2 rows twice more—36 (40) sts.

Hood
Work even on 36 (40) sts until hood measures 9 (10)"/23 (25.5)cm from beg. Divide sts evenly between 2 dpns.

FINISHING
Join hood seam using the Kitchener st.

Hood band

With RS facing and dpns, pick up and k 55 (61) sts evenly spaced around entire edge. Work back and forth in k1, p1 rib for 2 rows. Bind off loosely in rib. Overlap right band over left and sew to neck edge (see photo).

Hand slit edging

With RS facing and dpns, beg at bottom edge and pick up and k 30 (34) sts evenly spaced around entire edge. Turn and bind off knitwise.

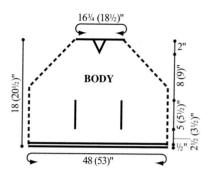

16¾ (18½)"

2"

BODY

8 (9)"

18 (20½)"

5 (5½)"

3½ (3½)"

48 (53)"

½"

2½ (3½)"

Create a special set to pass down from generation to generation. The cardigan is knit in one piece to the underarm and features a handsome Fair Isle pattern across the body. Designed by Karen Connor.

SIZES

Cardigan instructions are written for size 4. Changes for 6, 8 and 10 are in parentheses. Mitten instructions are written for size 4-6. Changes for 8-10 are in parentheses.

KNITTED MEASUREMENTS

Cardigan
▥ Chest (buttoned) 25 (28, 31, 33)"/63.5 (71, 78.5, 84)cm
▥ Length 12½ (14, 15, 16)"/31.5 (35.5, 38, 40.5)cm
▥ Upper arm 11 (13, 14, 15)"/28 (33, 35.5, 38)cm
Mitten
▥ Hand width 3 (3½)"/7.5 (9)cm
▥ Hand length 6 (7)"/15 (17.5)cm

MATERIALS

▥ 3 (4, 5, 5) 1¾oz/50g skeins (each approx 175yd/160m) of Koigu Wool Designs *Premium Merino* (wool②) in #2350.5 lt green (MC)
▥ 2 (2, 3, 3) skeins in #2343 dk green (CC)
▥ One pair each sizes 2 and 3 (2.5 and 3mm) needles *or size to obtain gauge*
▥ Sizes 2 and 3 (2.5 and 3mm) circular needles, 24"/60cm long

▥ One set (4) size 3 (3mm) dpn
▥ Stitch holder
▥ Stitch marker
▥ Five (6, 6, 6) ⅝"/16mm buttons

GAUGES

▥ 28 sts and 40 rows to 5"/12.5cm over St st using larger needles.
▥ 35 sts and 39 rows to 5"/12.5cm over St st and chart pat using larger needles.
Take time to check gauges.

Notes I Body is worked in one piece to armhole, then both fronts and back are worked separately to shoulder. **2** When changing colors, twist yarns on WS to prevent holes in work.

BODY

With smaller circular needle and CC, cast on 154 (174, 186, 198) sts. Work in p2, k2 rib for 2"/5cm, inc 15 (19, 19, 19) sts evenly spaced across last row and end with a WS row—169 (193, 205, 217) sts. Change to larger circular needle and St st.
Beg chart pat
Row I (RS) Work sts 12-st rep (sts 1-12) 14 (16, 17, 18) times, then work st 13 once. Cont to foll chart in this way until row 39 is completed. Work even with MC only, work even until piece measures 7½ (8, 8½, 9)"/19 (20, 21.5, 23)cm from beg, end with a WS row.
Separate for fronts and back
Next row (RS) Work 39 (45, 48, 51) sts and place on holder for right front, bind

off 7 sts for armhole, work until there are 77 (89, 95, 101) sts for back, leave rem sts unworked for left front. Change to larger straight needles and cont to work back sts until armhole measures 5 (6, 6½, 7)"/12.5 (15, 16.5, 17.5)cm, end with a WS row. Bind off.

Return to 39 (45, 48, 51) sts on right front and work even until armhole measures 3½ (4½, 5, 5½) "/9 (11.5, 12.5, 14)cm, end with a WS row.
Neck shaping
Next row (RS) Bind off 10 (11, 12, 12) sts, work to end. **Next row** Purl. **Next (dec) row (RS)** K4, ssk, work to end. **Next row** Purl. Rep these last 2 rows 7 times more—21 (26, 28, 31) sts. Work even until armhole measures same as back, end with a WS row. Bind off.

Join MC to rem sts and bind off 7 sts for armhole. Cont as for right front to neck shaping, end with a RS row.
Neck shaping
Next row (WS) Bind off 10 (11, 12, 12) sts, work to end. **Next (dec) row (RS)** Work to within last 6 sts, k2tog, k4. **Next row** Purl. Rep these last 2 rows 7 times more—21 (26, 28, 31) sts. Complete as for right front.

With smaller straight needles and CC, cast on 46 (46, 50, 54) sts. Work in k2, p2 rib for 2"/5cm, inc 8 (10, 10, 12) sts evenly spaced across last row and end with a WS row—54 (56, 60, 66) sts. Change to larger straight needles, MC and St st. Inc 1 st each side every 4th row 3 (12, 13, 13) times, every 6th row 9 (6, 6, 7) times—78 (92, 98, 106) sts. Work even until sleeve measures 10 (12, 13, 14)"/25.5 (30.5, 33, 35.5)cm from beg. Bind off.

Block pieces to measurements. Sew shoulder seams.
Neckband
With RS facing, smaller straight needles and CC, pick up and k 78 (82, 86, 86) sts along neck edge. Work in k2, p2 rib for 7 rows. Bind off loosely in rib.
Button band
With RS facing, smaller straight needles and CC, pick up and k 94 (106, 114, 122) sts evenly along left front edge. Work in k2, p2 rib for 7 rows. Bind off loosely in rib. Mark placement of 5 (6, 6, 6) buttons on band, with first and last ½"/1.5cm from top and bottom edges and 3 (4, 4, 4) spaced evenly between.
Buttonhole band
On right front, work as for buttonband until 2 rows of rib are completed. **Buttonhole row** *Work in rib to marker, bind off next 2 sts; rep from * to end. **Next row** Work in rib, casting on 2 sts over bound-off sts. Work in rib for 3 more rows, then bind off loosely in rib. Sew

sleeves into armholes, beg and end at center of bound-off sts. Sew sleeve seams. Sew on buttons.

RIGHT MITTEN

With dpn and CC, cast on 44 (48) sts. Divide sts between 3 dpn as foll: 14 (16) sts on first dpn, 16 sts on 2nd dpn and 14 (16) sts on 3rd dpn. Join and mark for beg of rnds. Work in k2, p2 rib for 2"/5cm. Change to MC and cont in St st for 5 (7) rnds.

Thumb

Inc rnd 1 K21 (22), M1, 4 (6), M1, k19 (20). **Next rnd** Knit. **Inc rnd 2** K21 (22), M1, k6 (8), M1, k19 (20). **Next rnd** Knit. Cont in this way, inc 2 sts for thumb every other rnd 3 times more—54 (58) sts. **Next rnd** K21 (22), leaving all sts on first dpn, cast on 1 st, k14 (16), cast on 1 st—16 (18) thumb sts. Place rem sts from 2nd dpn to 3rd dpn, leaving only thumb sts on 2nd dpn. Working back and forth in St st on 16 (18) thumb sts for 18 (22) rows, end with a WS row. **Next (dec) row** [K3tog] twice, [k2tog] 2 (3) times, [k3tog] twice—6 sts. Cut yarn leaving a long tail. Thread tail into tapestry needle and weave through sts. Pull tight to gather, fasten securely, then use tail to sew thumb seam.

Hand

Rejoin MC and pick up and k4 (6) sts along base of thumb, then complete rnd—44 (48) sts. Divide sts between 3 dpn as before. Work even for 25 (31) rnds.

Top shaping

Dec rnd 1 K1, SKP, k17 (19), k2tog, k1, SKP, k17 (19), k2tog—40 (44) sts. **Next rnd** Knit. **Dec rnd 1** K1, SKP, k15 (17), k2tog, k1, SKP, k15 (17), k2tog—36 (40) sts. **Next rnd** K. Cont in this way, dec 4 sts every other rnd until 20 sts rem. Cut yarn leaving a long tail. Thread tail into tapestry needle and weave through sts. Pull tight to gather, fasten off securely.

LEFT MITTEN

Work as for right mitten to thumb, then reverse thumb position as foll: **Inc rnd 1** K19 (20), m1, k4 (6), m1, k21 (22). When thumb is completed, cont as for right mitten to top shaping.

Top shaping

Dec rnd 1 K1, k2tog, k17 (19), SKP, k1, k2tog, k17 (19), SKP—40 (44) sts. **Next rnd** Knit. **Dec rnd 1** K1, k2tog, k15 (17), SKP, k1, k2tog, k15 (17), SKP—36 (40) sts. **Next rnd** Knit. Complete same as for right mitten.

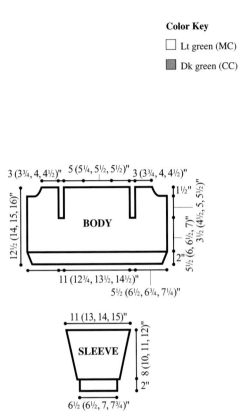

Color Key

☐ Lt green (MC)

■ Dk green (CC)

BODY

3 (3¾, 4, 4½)"   5 (5¼, 5½, 5½)"   3 (3¾, 4, 4½)"

12½ (14, 15, 16)"

1½"

5½ (6, 6½, 7)"
3½ (4½, 5, 5½)"

2"

11 (12¾, 13½, 14½)"

5½ (6½, 6¾, 7¼)"

SLEEVE

11 (13, 14, 15)"

8 (10, 11, 12)"

2"

6½ (6½, 7, 7¾)"

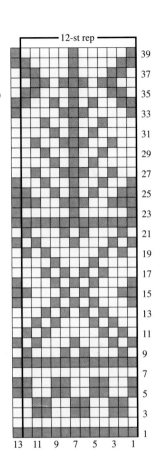

12-st rep

39
37
35
33
31
29
27
25
23
21
19
17
15
13
11
9
7
5
3
1

13 11 9 7 5 3 1

Bright colors in a cool cotton yarn are perfect for summer play days. Easy, knit-in fish motif is embroidered with French knots. Designed by Mary Bonnette of The Sassy Skein.

Instructions are written for size 4. Changes for 6, 8 and 10 are in parentheses.

▪ Chest 27 (29, 31, 32)"/70 (73.5, 78.5, 81)cm

▪ Length 14½ (15½, 16½, 17½)"/37 (39, 42, 44.5)

▪ Upper arm 10 (11, 12, 13)"25.5 (28, 30.5, 33)cm

▪ 3 (3, 4, 4) 1¾oz/50g balls (each approx 86yd/79m) of Schoeller Esslinger/ Skacel *Bermuda* (cotton/acrylic④) each in #17 orange (A) and #18 pink (B)

▪ 1 ball in #20 aqua (C)

▪ 1 (1, 2, 2) balls in #15 yellow (D)

▪ Small amount of black yarn

▪ One pair size 7 (4.5mm) needles *or size to obtain gauge*

▪ Size 7 (4.5mm) circular needle, 16"/40cm long

▪ Stitch holders

▪ Bobbins

18 sts and 20 rows to 4"/10cm over St st using size 7 (4.5mm) needles.
Take time to check gauge.

Notes I Do not carry yarns across. **2** Wind A, C and D onto bobbins. **3** Work fish motif with separate bobbins. **4** When changing colors, twist yarn on WS to prevent holes in work.

(over an even number of sts)
Row I (RS) *K1, p1; rep from * to end.
Row 2 K the purl sts and p the knit sts.
Rep row 2 for seed st.

With A, cast on 62 (66, 70, 74) sts. Work in seed st for 4 rows. Cont in St st until piece measures 14½ (15½, 16½, 17½)"/37 (39, 42, 44.5)cm from beg, end with a WS row.

Neck and shoulder shaping
Next row (RS) Bind off 14 (16, 17, 19) sts, k 34 (34, 36, 36) sts for back neck and place on a holder, bind off rem 14 (16, 17, 19) sts.

With B, work as for back until piece measures 6½ (7½, 8½, 9½)"/16.5 (19, 21.5, 24)cm from beg, end with a WS row.
Beg chart
Row I (RS) Work 14 (16, 18, 20) sts with B, work 34 sts of chart, then work 14 (16, 18, 20) sts with a separate ball of B. Cont as established to row 27. Then cont with B

only until piece measures 13 (14, 15, 16)"/33 (35.5, 38, 40.5)cm from beg, end with a WS row.

Neck shaping

Next row (RS) Work 17 (19, 20, 22) sts, place 28 (28, 30, 30) sts on a holder for front neck, join another ball of yarn and work to end. Working both sides at once, dec 1 st from each neck edge every row 3 times—14 (16,17, 19) sts each side. Work even until same length as back. Bind off sts each side for shoulder.

SLEEVES

With D, cast on 40 (46, 50, 54) sts. Work in seed st for 4 rows. **Next row (RS)** K across, inc 4 sts evenly spaced—44 (50, 54, 58) sts. Beg with a p row, cont in St st until piece measures 3¼ (3¾, 4¼, 4¾)"/8 (9.5, 10.5, 12)cm from beg. Bind off.

FINISHING

Block pieces to measurements. Sew shoulder seams.

Neckband

With RS facing, circular needle and B pick up and k 72 (72, 76, 76) sts evenly around neck. Join and work in seed st for 2 rnds. Bind off loosely in seed st.

Embroidery

With black yarn, work a French knot for eye. With C, B and D, work French knots for spots on fish; see photo for color placement. Place markers at 5 (5½, 6, 6½)"/12.5 (14, 15, 16.5)cm down from shoulders. Sew sleeves to armholes between markers. Sew side and sleeve seams.

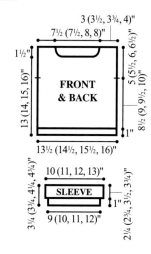

3 (3½, 3¾, 4)"

7½ (7½, 8, 8)"

1½"

13 (14, 15, 16)"

5 (5½, 6, 6½)"

8½ (9, 9½, 10)"

FRONT & BACK

1"

13½ (14½, 15½, 16)"

10 (11, 12, 13)"

3¼ (3¾, 4¼, 4¾)"

SLEEVE

1"

2¼ (2¾, 3½, 3¾)"

9 (10, 11, 12)"

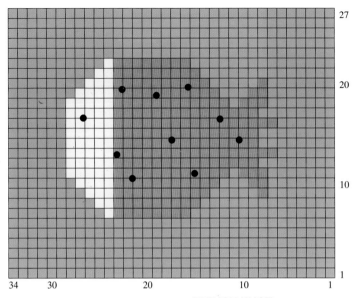

FRENCH KNOT

Color Key

■ Orange (A)

■ Lt Blue (C)

□ Yellow (C)

● French knot

Black seed stitch borders accent the bold knit-in gingham plaid. Embroider cherries and stems in Duplicate stitch for a playful touch. Designed by Gayle Bunn.

SIZES

Instructions are written for size 4. Changes for 6 and 8 are in parentheses.

KNITTED MEASUREMENTS

▥ Chest 28 (31½, 35)"/71 (80, 89)cm
▥ Length 14½ (15½, 16½)"/37 (39, 42)cm
▥ Upper arm 12 (13, 14)"/30.5 (33, 35.5)cm

MATERIALS

▥ 3 (4, 5) 1¾oz/50g balls (each approx 136yd/125m) of Patons® *Grace* (cotton③) in #60040 black (A)
▥ 3 (3, 4) balls in #60005 white (B)
▥ 1 ball each in #60705 red (C) and #60527 green (D)
▥ One pair each sizes 3 and 6 (3.25 and 4mm) needles *or size to obtain gauge*
▥ Stitch holders

GAUGE

24 sts and 28 rows to 4"/10cm over St st and chart using size 6 (4mm) needles. *Take time to check gauge.*

Notes I When changing colors, twist yarn on WS to prevent holes in work. **2** Cherries, leaves and stems are embroidered on after pieces are knitted.

SEED STITCH

(multiple of 2 sts plus 1)
Row I *K1, p1; rep from *, end k1.
Row 2 K the purl sts and p the knit sts.
Rep row 2 for seed st.

BACK

With smaller needles and A, cast on 85 (95, 105) sts. Work in seed st for 8 rows, end with a WS row. Change to larger needles.

Beg side slits and chart pat

Row I (RS) Work 5 sts in seed st with A, working in St st, beg chart at st 1 and work to st 20, then work sts 11-20 for 5 (6, 7) times, work sts 21-25, then work 5 sts in seed st with A. Keeping 5 sts each side in seed st, work as established until row 12 of chart has been completed, end with a WS row. Cont in St st only as foll.

Re-establish chart pat

Row I (RS) Beg with st 6 of chart, work to st 20, then work sts 11-20 for 6 (7, 8) times, then work sts 21-30 once. Cont to foll chart and work even until piece measures 8½ (9, 9½)"/21.5 (23, 24)cm from beg, end with a WS row.

Armhole shaping

Bind off 5 (5, 5) sts at beg of next 2 rows—75 (85, 95) sts. Work even until armhole measures 6 (6½, 7)"/15 (16.5, 17.5)cm, end with a WS row.

Neck and shoulder shaping

Bind off 10 (13, 15) sts at beg of next 2 rows, 11 (13, 15) sts at beg of next 2 rows. Place rem 33 (33, 35) sts on a holder for back neck.

FRONT

Work as for back until armhole measures 1 (1½, 2)"/2.5 (4, 5)cm, end with a WS row.

Right placket and neck shaping

Next row (RS) Foll chart, work 35 (40, 45) sts, place on a holder for left front, then work 5 sts in seed st with A (placket), foll chart work to end. Keeping 5 sts in seed st, work as established until armhole measures 3½ (4, 4½)"/9 (10, 11.5)cm, end with a WS row. **Next row (RS)** Work 11 sts, place on a holder for right neck, work to end. Dec 1 st at neck edge every row 6 (6, 7) times, every other row twice—21 (26, 30) sts. Work even until armhole measures same as back, end with a WS row.

Right shoulder shaping

At right armhole edge, bind off 10 (13, 15) sts once, then 11 (13, 15) sts once.

Left placket and neck shaping

Place sts from holder back on LH needle, then cast on 5 sts with A (placket)—40 (45, 50) sts. **Next row (WS)** Work 5 sts in seed st with A, foll chart work to end. Cont to work as for right front, reversing neck and shoulder shaping.

SLEEVES

With smaller needles and A, cast on 49 (51, 53) sts. Work in seed st for 8 rows, inc 1 st at end of last row and end with a WS row—50 (52, 54) sts. Change to larger needles and St st.

Beg chart

Row 1 (RS) Beg with st 6 (5, 4) of chart, work to st 20, then work sts 11-20 for 3 times, work sts 21-25 (21-26, 21-27) once. Cont as established for 3 more rows, end with a WS row. Inc 1 st each side (working incs into pat) on next row, then every 4th row 10 (12, 14) times more—72 (78, 84) sts. Work even until sleeve measures 11 (12, 13)"/28 (30.5, 33)cm from beg, end with a WS row. Bind off.

FINISHING

Block pieces to measurements.

Embroidery

Count 20 rows down from base of placket, then mark 15 center sts. Embroider motif in duplicate st foll chart. With C, outline each cherry with outline stitches. With D, embroider stems in backstitch. Sew shoulder seams.

Collar

With RS facing, smaller needles and A, work first 5 sts from right neck holder in seed st, k next 6 sts, pick up and k 12 (14-15) sts evenly along right neck edge, k33 (33, 35) sts from back neck holder, k12 (14, 15) sts evenly along left neck edge, k 6 sts from left neck holder, then work last 5 sts in seed st—79 (83, 87) sts. Work in seed st for 3¼ (3½, 4)"/8 (9, 10) cm. Bind off loosely in seed st. Lap left placket under right and sew bottom edge in place. Sew sleeves to armholes. Sew sleeve seams. Sew side seams to side slits.

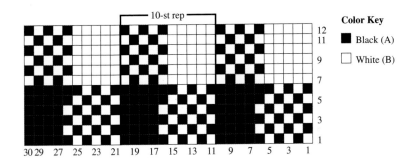

Color Key

■ Black (A)

☐ White (B)

10-st rep

12
11
9
7
5
3
1

30 29 27 25 23 21 19 17 15 13 11 9 7 5 3 1

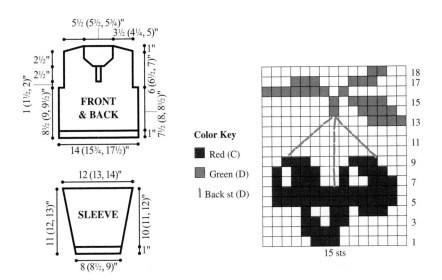

5½ (5½, 5¾)"
3½ (4¼, 5)"
1"
2½"
2½"
1 (1½, 2)"
6 (6½, 7)"
8½ (9, 9½)"
7½ (8, 8½)"
1"

FRONT & BACK

14 (15¾, 17½)"

12 (13, 14)"

SLEEVE

11 (12, 13)"
10 (11, 12)"
1"
8 (8½, 9)"

Color Key

■ Red (C)

■ Green (D)

| Back st (D)

18
17
15
13
11
9
7
5
3
1

15 sts

85

TURTLE PULLOVER

Slow and steady...

Intarsia-knit turtles are outlined with chain stitch, while green suede or felt fabric spots are sewn to the backs to create a three-dimensional effect. Designed by Amy Bahrt.

SIZES

Instructions are written for size 4. Changes for 6 and 8 are in parentheses.

KNITTED MEASUREMENTS

- Chest 29 (31, 33)"/73.5 (78.5, 84)cm
- Length (with edge rolled) 14½ (15½, 16½)"/37 (39, 42)cm
- Upper arm 12½ (13½, 14½)"/31.5 (34, 37)cm

MATERIALS

- 2 (2, 3) 3½oz/100g skeins (each approx 183yd/167m) of Tahki Yarns/Tahki•Stacy Charles, Inc. *Donegal Tweed* (wool④) each in #822 dk blue (A) and #823 lt blue (B)
- 1 skein each in #878 dk green (C) and #803 lt green (D)
- One pair size 7 (4.5mm) needles *or size to obtain gauge*
- Size 5 (3.75mm) circular needle, 16"/40cm long
- Size F/5 (3.75mm) crochet hook
- Stitch holders
- Bobbins
- Red embroidery floss
- 3½"/9cm square of dk green suede
- Dk blue sewing thread
- Small amount of polyester fiberfill

GAUGE

17 sts and 24 rows to 4"/10cm over St st using size 7 (4.5mm) needles.
Take time to check gauge.

Notes I Do not carry yarns across more than 5 sts. **2** Wind yarn onto bobbins. Work each turtle motif with separate bobbins and use separate bobbins for background colors. **3** When changing colors, twist yarn on WS to prevent holes in work.

STRIPE PATTERN

Work 12 rows A and 12 rows B. Rep these 24 rows for stripe pat.

FRONT

With A (A, B), cast on 62 (66, 70) sts. Work in St st for 6 (8, 12) rows. Cont in stripe pat until 3 rows of 1st (1st, 2nd) B stripe have been completed, end with a RS row.

Beg chart pat

Row I (WS) Work 6 (8, 10) sts with B, work 14 sts of chart, 22 sts with B, 14 sts of chart, 6 (8, 10) sts with B. Cont stripe pat and motif placement as established through row 24 of chart. **Row 25 (WS)** Work 6 (8, 10) sts with B, 14 sts of chart, 4 sts with B, 14 sts of chart beg on row 1, 4 sts with B, 14 sts of chart, 6 (8, 10) sts of B. Cont as established through row 30 of center motif chart, then cont stripe pat until 4 (8, 10) rows of 4th A stripe have been completed, end with a WS row. Piece should measure approx 13½ (14½, 15½)" from beg.

Neck shaping

Next row (RS) Work 25 (27, 28) sts, place 12 (12, 14) sts on a holder for front neck, join another skein of yarn and work to end. Working both sides at once, bind off 2 sts from each neck edge twice, then dec 1 st at each neck edge every other row 3 times—18 (20, 21) sts each side. Work even until piece measures 15½ (16½, 17½)"/39 (42, 44.5)cm from beg, end with a WS row. Bind off sts each side for shoulders.

BACK

Work as for front (omitting chart), until piece measures same length as front to shoulder, end with a WS row.

Neck and shoulder shaping

Bind off 18 (20, 21) sts, then k 26 (26, 28) sts for back neck and place on a holder, bind off rem 18 (20, 21) sts.

SLEEVES

With A (A, B), cast on 32 (32, 34) sts. Work even in St st for 6 (0-12) rows. Cont in stripe pat and AT THE SAME TIME, inc 1 st each side every 4th row 0 (1, 2) times, every 6th row 11 (12, 12) times—54 (58, 62) sts. Work even until piece measures 13 (14, 15)"/33 (35.5, 38)cm from beg, end with a WS row. Bind off.

FINISHING

Block pieces lightly to measurements, allowing lower edges of pieces to roll as in photo. Sew shoulder seams.

Neckband

With RS facing, circular needle and A, pick up and k 72 (72, 76) sts evenly around neck. Join and work in k1, p1 rib for 1"/2.5cm, then work in St st for 1"/2.5cm. Bind off loosely.

Turtle motifs

With D outline each turtle shell with a line of chain stitches. Cut 6 suede spots foll template. Referring to photo for placement, use thread to sew to turtle shells using blanket stitches and stuffing lightly with fiberfill. With D, work a French knot for each eye. With red floss, work a single chain stitch for each tongue.

Tails

(make 3)

With crochet hook and C, ch for 1"/2.5cm. Fasten off. Sew each tail to center bottom of turtle shell as shown. Place markers at 6¼ (6¾, 7¼)"/16 (17, 18.5)cm down from shoulders. Sew sleeves to armholes between markers. Sew side and sleeve seams.

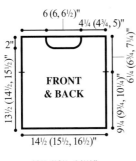

6 (6, 6½)"

4¼ (4¾, 5)"

2"

13½ (14½, 15½)"

FRONT & BACK

9¼ (9¾, 10¼)"

6¼ (6¾, 7¼)"

14½ (15½, 16½)"

12½ (13½, 14½)"

13 (14, 15)"

SLEEVE

12 (14, 13)"

1 (0, 2)"

7½ (7½, 8)"

Color Key

■ Dk blue (A)

■ Lt blue (B)

■ Dk green (C)

■ Lt green (D)

● French knot

∨ Chain st

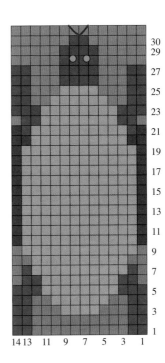

30
29
27
25
23
21
19
17
15
13
11
9
7
5
3
1

14 13 11 9 7 5 3 1

This versatile V-neck rib and seed stitch pullover with single pocket and drawstring hem is equally stylish on a little girl or boy. Designed by Mary Bonnette of The Sassy Skein.

SIZES

Instructions are written for size 4. Changes for 6, 8 and 10 are in parentheses.

KNITTED MEASUREMENTS

▨ Chest 27 (28, 31, 33)"/68.5 (71, 78.5, 84)cm

▨ Length 13 (14, 15, 16)"/33 (35.5, 38, 40.5)cm

▨ Upper arm 10 (12, 13, 14)"/25.5 (30.5, 33, 35.5)cm

MATERIALS

▨ 1 (2, 2, 2) 4¼oz/125g hanks (each approx 256yd/234m) of Classic Elite Yarns *Provence* (cotton) each in #2627 red (MC) and #2616 ecru (A)

▨ 1 hank in #2610 navy (B)

▨ One pair size 10½ (6.5mm) needles *or size to obtain gauge*

▨ Size 10 (6mm) circular needle, 20"/51cm long

▨ One set (4) size 5 (3.75mm) dpn

▨ Stitch marker

GAUGE

13 sts and 20 rows to 4"/10cm over rib pat using size 10½ (6.5mm) needles and 2 strands of yarn.

Take time to check gauge.

Notes 1 Use 2 strands of yarn held tog throughout unless otherwise stated. **2** Sew pieces tog using 1 strand of yarn. **3** Drawstring casing is worked in one piece, then front and back are worked separately.

RIB PATTERN STITCH

(multiple of 3 sts plus 2)
Row 1 (RS) *K2, p1; rep from *, end k2.
Row 2 P across.
Rep rows 1 and 2 for rib pat.

SEED STITCH

(multiple of 2 sts plus 1)
Row 1 *K1, p1; rep from *, end k1.
Row 2 K the purl sts and p the knit sts.
Rep row 2 for seed st.

DRAWSTRING CASING

With circular needle and A, cast on 86 (90, 98, 106) sts. Join and pm for beg of rnds. **Rnds 1-5** Knit. **Rnd 6** (turning ridge) Purl. **Rnd 7** Knit. **Rnd 8** (eyelets) K19 (20, 22, 24), yo, k2tog, k1, yo, k2tog, work to end. **Rnds 9 and 10** Knit.

FRONT

With MC and straight needles, work row 1 of rib pat across first 43 (45, 49, 53) sts, inc 1 (2, 1, 0) st(s) evenly spaced across— 44 (47, 50, 53) sts. Leave rem sts on circular needle for back. Cont in rib pat until piece measures 9 (9½, 10, 11)"/23 (24, 25.5, 28)cm above turning ridge, end with a WS row.
Separate for V-neck
Keeping to pat st, work across first 22 (23,

25, 26) sts, join another 2 strands of MC and bind off 0 (1, 0, 1) center st, work to end. Working both sides at once, dec 1 st from each neck edge every other row 9 (10, 11, 11) times—13 (13, 14, 15) sts each side. Work even until piece measures 13 (14, 15, 16)"/33 (35.5, 38, 40.5)cm above turning ridge, end with WS row. Bind off each side.

With straight needles and B, work row 1 of rib pat across rem 43 (45, 49, 53) sts, inc 1 (2, 1, 0) sts evenly spaced across— 44 (47, 50, 53) sts. Cont in rib pat and work for 4 more rows, end with a RS row.

Stripe Pat

Work *1 row MC, 5 rows A, 1 row MC and 5 rows B; rep from * once more, then work 1 row MC. With A only, work even until piece measures same as front, end with a WS row.

Neck and shoulder shaping

Bind off 13 (13, 14, 15) sts at beg of next 2 rows. Bind off rem 18 (21, 22, 23) sts for back neck. Sew shoulder seams. Place markers at 5 (6, 6½, 7)"/12.5 (15, 16.5, 17.5)cm down from shoulders.

SLEEVES

With RS facing, straight needles and MC, pick up and k 35 (41, 44, 47) sts evenly spaced between armhole markers. Beg with row 2, work in rib pat for 3 rows, end with a WS row. Dec 1 st each side every 8th (6th, 6th, 6th) row 4 (6, 6, 8) times, AT

THE SAME TIME, when piece measures 3½ (4, 4, 4½)"/9 (10, 10, 11.5)cm from beg, end with a WS row.

Stripe pat

Work 5 rows B, 1 row MC, 5 (5, 7, 7) rows A, 1 row MC and 5 rows B. Cont with MC until piece measures 10 (11, 12, 13)"/25.5 (28, 30.5, 33)cm from beg, dec 4 (4, 5, 4)sts evenly spaced across last row and end with a WS row—23 (25, 27, 27) sts.

Cuff

Working in seed st, work 2 rows B, 2 rows A and 1 row MC. Bind off in seed st with A.

POCKET

With straight needles and B, cast on 14 (14, 17, 17) sts. Cont in rib pat and work even for 5 rows, end with a RS row.

STRIPE PAT

Work 1 row MC, 5 (5, 7, 7) rows A, 1 row MC, 5 rows B and 1 row MC. With A, bind off purlwise.

FINISHING

Lightly block pieces to measurements.

Neckband

With RS facing, circular needle and A, pick up and k 57 (65, 71, 71) sts. Do not join. Work back and forth in seed st for 3 (3, 4, 4) rows. Bind off loosely in seed st. Overlap right neckband over left and sew to neck edge, as shown. Sew side and sleeves seams. Fold drawstring casing to WS along turning ridge and sew in place. Sew on pocket, as shown.

I-cord drawstring

With 1 strand of B and dpn, cast on 2 sts. Work in I-cord as foll: ***Next row (RS)** With 2nd dpn, k2, do *not* turn. Slide sts back to beg of needle to work next row from RS; rep from * until I-cord measures 38 (39, 42, 44)"/96.5 (99, 106.5, 112.5)cm from beg. Cut yarn leaving a long tail. Thread tail into tapestry needle, then weave needle through sts; fasten off. Weave drawstring through casing. Knot drawstring ends.

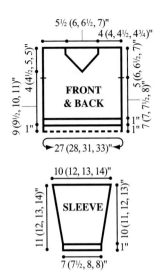

5½ (6, 6½, 7)"

4 (4, 4½, 4¾)"

9 (9½, 10, 11)"

4 (4½, 5, 5)"

FRONT & BACK

5 (6, 6½, 7)"

7 (7, 7½, 8)"

1"

1"

1"

27 (28, 31, 33)"

10 (12, 13, 14)"

11 (12, 13, 14)"

SLEEVE

10 (11, 12, 13)"

1"

7 (7½, 8, 8)"

RESOURCES

CANADIAN RESOURCES

Write to US resources for mail-order availability of yarns not listed.

BERROCO, INC.
distributed by
S. R. Kertzer, Ltd.

CLASSIC ELITE YARNS
distributed by
S. R. Kertzer, Ltd.

DIAMOND YARN
9697 St. Laurent
Montreal, PQ H3L 2N1
and
155 Martin Ross, Unit #3
Toronto, ON M3J 2L9

KOIGU WOOL DESIGNS
R R #1
Williamsford, ON N0H 2V0

**LES FILS MUENCH,
CANADA**
5640 Rue Valcourt
Brossard, Quebec J4W 1C5
Muenchcan@videotron.ca

MISSON FALLS
PO Box 224
Consecon, ON K0K 1T0

PATONS®
PO Box 40
Listowel, ON N4W 3H3

ROWAN
distributed by
Diamond Yarn

SCHOELLER ESSLINGER
distributed by
Diamond Yarn

UK RESOURCES

Not all yarns used in this book are available in the UK. For yarns not available, make a comparable substitute or contact the US manufacturer for purchasing and mail-order information.

ROWAN YARNS
Green Lane Mill
Holmfirth
West Yorks HD7 1RW
Tel: 01484-681881

SILKSTONE
12 Market Place
Cockermouth
Cumbria, CA13 9NQ
Tel: 01900-821052

**THOMAS RAMSDEN
GROUP**
Netherfield Road
Guiseley
West Yorks LS20 9PD
Tel: 01943-872264

VOGUE KNITTING KIDS KNITS

Editor-in-Chief
TRISHA MALCOLM

Editorial Coordinator
MICHELLE LO

Art Director
CHI LING MOY

Photography
**JACK DEUTSCH STUDIOS
EYE[4]MEDIA**

Executive Editor
CARLA S. SCOTT

Book Manager
THERESA MCKEON

Knitting Editor
JEAN GUIRGUIS

Production Manager
DAVID JOINNIDES

Instructions Editors
**KAREN GREENWALD
PAT HARSTE**

■

Yarn Editor
VERONICA MANNO

President, Sixth&Spring Books
ART JOINNIDES

LOOK FOR THESE OTHER TITLES IN
THE VOGUE ON THE GO SERIES...

■